Public Relations & Ethics

a bibliography

Public Relations & Ethics

a bibliography

John P. Ferré

and

Shirley C. Willihnganz

G.K. Hall & Co.
70 Lincoln Street, Boston, Massachusetts

First published 1991
by G.K. Hall & Co.
70 Lincoln Street
Boston, Massachusetts 02111

10 9 8 7 6 5 4 3 2 1

Library of Congress Cataloging-in-Publication Data

Ferré, John P.
  Public relations & ethics: a bibliography / John P. Ferré, Shirley C.
Willihnganz.
        p. cm.
    Includes bibliographical references and index.
    ISBN 0-8161-7255-2
    1. Public relations – Bibliography. 2. Public relations consultants
 – Professional ethics – Bibliography. 3. Public relations consultants
 – Professional ethics – United States. I. Willihnganz, Shirley C.
  II. Title. III. Title: Public relations and ethics.
  Z7164.P957F47   1991
  [HM263]
  016.6592 – dc20
                                                          91-3781
                                                          CIP

The paper used in this publication meets the minimum requirements of
American National Standard for Information Sciences – Permanence of
Paper for Printed Library Materials. ANSI Z39.48-1984.   ∞™
MANUFACTURED IN THE UNITED STATES OF AMERICA

Contents

Foreword

Dean Kruckeberg, Ph.D.
PRSA Fellow
Coordinator,
Public Relations Degree Program
University of Northern Iowa

The day this foreword was being written, allied coalition forces were continuing to pummel Iraq with nonstop air strikes. The bombings were surgically precise, apparently able to destroy military targets while safeguarding from destruction the predominantly civilian areas of Iraq. But the numbers of these sorties increased geometrically throughout the war to a saturation point far beyond most Americans' ability to comprehend.

Certainly, Iraq was being destroyed, perhaps – and more than we were prepared to admit – in a manner akin to the Iraqis' ravaging of Kuwait. Yet despite this mass destruction and its inevitable loss of human life, we confidently assured ourselves that our motives were pure and that our efforts to prevent at least civilian casualties were admirable, if not totally successful.

Such air strikes also meant that the allied coalition would not have to suffer the predicted immense casualties of a sustained ground war. And, certainly, our involvement in this war was by far a lesser evil than what would have loomed if Saddam's ambitions had been left unchecked.

Indeed, it was clear to the majority of Americans that, unlike the uncomfortable questions about our involvement in Vietnam, our military objectives in the Persian Gulf were both necessary and just; we were behaving responsibly and ethically, and Operation Desert Storm was, without doubt, a noble cause.

What does this horrendous war have to do with public relations ethics? At first appearance, perhaps nothing; but, in reality, perhaps everything. Both sides, in their own minds, were able to justify this conflict as a "holy war"–if not literally, at least figuratively–in which they were fighting for principles that transcended political self-interest. When asked, both sides replied–in apparent sincerity–that they were acting ethically and morally.

Too, Operation Desert Storm was the result of failed diplomacy, as all wars are; but–at an even more basic level–it was a direct result of obviously disparate senses of ethics and morality. These disparate senses were explicable in part because of the failures of those from different cultures and geopolitical perspectives to communicate and to concur in their perceptions of what is right and what is wrong in a global community of diverse peoples living in a world shrinking in both time and space.

As the Persian Gulf War has dramatically illustrated, the ramifications of decisions and actions made anywhere throughout the world in this decade before the twenty-first century can only increase, and they will do so exponentially through the impact of new technologies and related phenomena, whether they are manifested in sophisticated satellite telecommunication systems or in Patriot missiles. Without a doubt, questions of ethics and morality will become even more complex in tomorrow's world, and their resolutions will become even more consequential in their application.

Tomorrow's practice of public relations most assuredly will be different from today's and far more critical because–now more than ever–we must attempt to live in harmony with our neighbors and within our global environment, or else we all shall perish.

People must seek closer intimacy and understanding with their fellow humans throughout the world for economic, political, and social reasons, among others. They must behave ethically and morally because the impact of unethical and immoral behavior will be exponentially more harmful to increasing numbers of people.

Many–probably most–public relations practitioners, working for a pervasive range of transnational organizations, will be communicating with those in social systems and cultures far different from their own and with those having different senses and standards of ethics and morality.

Thus, any understanding of, appreciation for, and consensus about public relations ethics certainly will be all the more challenging in the future as our society grows increasingly complex and particularly as the "global village," the world community, becomes ever smaller through new means of communication and transportation.

Before we grapple with tomorrow's ethical problems in public relations, however, we must sufficiently appreciate that existing codes of public relations ethics are hardly up to the task of providing a comprehensive and appropriate basis for resolving the ethical questions of the present–let alone of addressing future questions that will arise within an emerging global society and perhaps a new world order.

It is the challenge of today's public relations scholars and practitioners to examine and attempt to address the ethical issues that exist today as well as those that will evolve in the future to perplex practitioners and the organizations they represent.

Much work remains to be done; indeed, this Herculean task has yet to be even duly considered. Continuing development of relevant and useful codes of ethics will require an examination of the philosophical foundations of the basic constructs of ethics themselves as well as a thorough reexamination of the definition and role of public relations as the profession is developing globally and as it will be practiced worldwide.

Indeed, public relations practitioners and scholars, through their professional organizations, will have to pursue actively the continuing development of codes of ethics, including specific addenda to their existing codes that must take into consideration the exigencies of evolving worldwide norms in public relations practice. Professional organizations should strive to communicate with their counterparts regionally and worldwide in an attempt to come to a consensus in their codes with the ultimate goal of developing a multilaterally honored code of ethics that public relations professionals worldwide endorse and follow.

But this overwhelming mandate – with its need to search for cultural universals in ethics – is putting a large cart before a minuscule horse. Much needs to be done at the most basic level, particularly by scholars who have a particular mission. Much more research on codes of ethics must be placed on the scholarly agenda, with the ultimate aim of having valid and reliable data codified and made available that can help achieve these ambitious ends.

Equally important, public relations educators must instill in their students a thorough understanding of and appreciation for ethics in public relations. Of course, this charge assumes ethics can indeed be taught – but certainly they can because ethics are a part of knowledge, and knowledge can be learned.

A perhaps more interesting questions is, can the academy make its students ethical, that is, in this context, moral? Can this behavioral expectation be considered the responsibility of the academy? If not, then of whom? So many questions exist in this critical area of public relations ethics. So much work needs to be done. That is why this book is a wonderful gift for those who recognize and accept the challenge of resolving the questions of public relations ethics.

This book begins with the provocative discussion of an intellectual task that Dietrich Bonhoeffer performed during another wartime era, World War II, when Bonhoeffer was imprisoned by the Nazis for plotting to assassinate Hitler. The authors skillfully use this point of departure to draw an interesting parallel between Bonhoeffer's analysis of truth-telling in terms of definition, method, and purpose and the sources of ethics in public relations.

The primary purpose and major content of this book is a comprehensive bibliography of every published English-language source on ethics and public relations. In performing this task, and performing it so well, the authors have saved public relations scholars and practitioners thousands of hours of research, and by so doing, they have fostered and encouraged scholarship and research in public relations ethics. For this, we owe them our immense gratitude.

Introduction

When Dietrich Bonhoeffer was writing "What Is Meant by 'Telling the Truth'?" he was not thinking about public relations at all. It was 1945, and he had been imprisoned for two years awaiting execution by the Nazis for plotting to assassinate Adolf Hitler. Writing on scraps of paper in his prison cell in Tagel, Bonhoeffer was trying to finish his book on how to perceive the right course of action in concrete historical circumstances. Honesty was on his mind in the spring when he was hanged.

Although Bonhoeffer did not live to complete his chapter on telling the truth – the book comes to an abrupt, disconcerting end – what he did complete continues to intrigue its readers. The following example illustrates Bonhoeffer's thinking:

> [A] teacher asks a child in front of the class whether it is true that his father often comes home drunk. It is true, but the child denies it. The teacher's question has placed him in a situation for which he is not yet prepared. He feels only that what is taking place is an unjustified interference in the order of the family and that he must oppose it. What goes on in the family is not for the ears of the class in school. The family has its own secret and must preserve it. The teacher has failed to respect the reality of this institution. The child ought now to find a way of answering which would comply with both the rule of the family and the rule of the school. But he is not yet able to do this. He lacks experience, knowledge, and the ability to express himself in the right way. As a simple no to the teacher's question the child's answer is certainly untrue; yet at the same time it nevertheless gives expression to the truth that the family is an institution sui generis and that the teacher had no right to interfere with it. The child's answer can indeed be called a lie; yet this lie contains more truth, that is to say, it is more in accordance with reality than would have been the case if the child had betrayed his father's weakness in front of the class. According to the measure of his knowledge the child acted correctly. The blame for the lie falls back entirely upon the teacher. An experienced man in the same position as the

1

child would have been able to correct his questioner's error while at the same time avoiding a formal untruth in his answer, and he would thus have found the "right word."[1]

In this passage, Bonhoeffer illustrated careful, contextual analysis of a plausible scenario. He deftly handled the definition of truthfulness, in this case distinguishing between narrow-minded literalism and broader symbolic meaning. This distinction suggests Bonhoeffer's ethical decision-making method. Although he believed that the precise contours of moral decisions could not be known in advance of the context in which decisions must be made, Bonhoeffer understood that they could be anticipated to some extent because truly moral decisions were those that enabled church, culture, government, and marriage and family to enhance human life. And as the boy in the example justifiably lied in order to protect his family from public scorn, all ethical decisions are purposeful, according to Bonhoeffer.

Although public relations was out of Bonhoeffer's purview, his analysis of truth-telling in terms of definition, method, and purpose parallels the sources in the ethics of public relations. Just as truthfulness differs between the child and the adult in Bonhoeffer's illustration, distinctions appear in the literature on public relations. No one advocates lying, but various rationales support everything from silence to full public disclosure, often depending upon the social context. Similarly, Bonhoeffer proposes a theological decision-making process in much the same way that various ethical decision-making methods appear subtly or overtly in the public relations literature. Furthermore, in the same way that Bonhoeffer proposes divine humaneness as the goal of theological ethics, the sources in the ethics of public relations propose democracy or professionalism or organizational and community enhancement as their goal. These parallels suggest that the ethics of public relations be understood as a subset of applied ethics, the study of enduring moral concerns in a specific historical context. Bonhoeffer would rightly encourage such deliberate analysis of the ethics of public relations because he found grand moral principles to be meaningless; moral decisions are always made in particular social circumstances.

Bonhoeffer's illustration applies in another fundamental way. As he was concerned with the meaning of telling the truth, so is the study of the ethics of public relations essentially an examination of the implications of truth-telling in a particular institutional context. The ethics of public relations can be understood as an arm of business ethics because public relations is most often employed by business to smooth relations between organizations and the communities with which they interact, but this concept is much too narrow, given that government, community groups, and churches use public relations as much as industry does. Instead, the ethics of public relations involves the definitions, methods, and purposes of truth-telling whenever individuals, organizations, or communities share information. To be sure, locating the ethics of public relations under the rubric of truth-telling requires a very broad account of what honesty means. But if there is any merit to the current approaches to public relations that stress the roles of counselor and intermediary between organization and community, then truth-telling is central to the enterprise.

PROCEDURE

The goal for this project was to locate every published English-language source on ethics and public relations. The study of communication ethics in general has been growing steadily since the Vietnam War, the industrialized world having entered the so-called information age early in that struggle, but the enterprise has been largely unsystematic. Although the field has two primary bibliographies, one by Clifford Christians and Vernon Jensen and the other by Thomas Cooper, their focus is on speech and mass communication, not on public relations.[2]

Finding the references was a matter primarily of searching a number of print sources and data bases. The search used "ethics" and the closely related key words "accountability," "morals," "responsibility," and "values." Along with "public relations" and "PR," we used the terms "community relations," "corporate advocacy," "issues management," and "public information." For those on-line sources that scan references, we listed Edward Bernays, Marvin Olasky, Michael Ryan, and Donald Wright as main authors. We searched through the following sources: ABI/Inform (1971 to present: indexes 800 publications in business and related fields), Business Periodicals Index (1958 to present: indexes 275 business periodicals), Dissertation Abstracts Online (1861 to present: lists every American dissertation accepted at an accredited institution), ERIC (1966 to present: indexes research reports and 700 periodicals of interest to education), Magazine Index (1959-1970; 1973 to present: indexes 435 popular magazines), PAIS International (1972 to present: indexes the public policy literature of business, economics, political science, and other social sciences), Philosopher's Index (1940 to present: indexes and abstracts books and articles from 270 journals of philosophy and related interdisciplinary fields), Social Scisearch (1972 to present: indexes 1,500 social science journals as well as social science articles in 3,000 journals in natural, physical, and biomedical sciences), Sociological Abstracts (1963 to present: indexes 1,600 serials in the social and behavioral sciences), Trade & Industry Index (1981 to present: indexes 300 trade and industry journals as well as business and trade articles in 1,200 other publications), and U.S. Political Science Documents (1975 to present: indexes 150 journals in political, social, and policy sciences). As we retrieved the relevant articles and books, we checked their bibliographies and footnotes if they had them to find sources that the search through indexes may have missed. We augmented this process by photocopying the file on ethics at the national office of the Public Relations Society of America and checked the references cited in academic papers and textbooks. By the end of this process, we were finding massive duplication, which suggested to us that we had located most of the available sources in print on the ethics of public relations.

This four-part search process – using on-line data bases, print indexes, references in articles and books, and sources from professionals and academics – was essential because the overlap between reference pools is unpredictable at best. Indexes often overlook rich sources of information such as newsletters, and they reference public relations sometimes under business, sometimes under communication, and sometimes as a discrete, independent category. The subcategory "public relations and ethics" often does not exist at all, and if it does, it may list sources that have little to do with the evaluation of PR from moral perspectives. The ethics of public relations is a disparate enterprise requiring the researcher to investigate diverse types of resources. We hope that we have simplified the task for future investigators.

We selected for reference all articles and books on public relations that focus on morals, values, and ethics. These three concepts are often used interchangeably, even though Western philosophers have made the following distinctions for millennia: *morality*: traditional rules or aspirations for behavior that bond and regulate the social order; *values*: objects, characteristics, or attitudes considered to be good; and *ethics*: systematic thinking about moral problems, judgments, and behavior. Although discussion of the ethics of public relations would become more subtle and discriminating if writers followed these distinctions more carefully, we have included references to articles concerning morality and values as well as ethics precisely because the terms are so commonly intertwined. We leave to future investigators the task of drawing the finer distinctions that can clarify the terms of argument in the field. What we have cited, without judgment of merit, are those printed sources that discuss public relations in terms of morality, values, and ethics in any of a myriad of ways. Breadth is called for at this nascent stage; we hope that increased sophistication will follow.

By casting the broadest possible net, we hope that this bibliography will serve three audiences. First are PR practitioners who may use this index to find sources that can help them solve the problems that they and their clients and employers face. Second are public relations educators, who should find a wealth of material to enrich their teaching and research. Finally, we hope that students of public relations can use these sources not just to write library research papers but also to perceive the dynamics of what being a public relations professional actually means. To serve practitioners, educators, and students, we have read and summarized every source, hoping that the brief and consistent annotations, together with the index, will ease the access to sources that will instruct, infuriate, and intrigue them.

A caveat is in order here. Our bibliography is limited to those sources that can be retrieved easily in any academic library with interlibrary loan services. Thus we do not cite convention papers or graduate theses unless they were subsequently published. Similarly, we do not cite book reviews – given the paucity of books on the ethics of public relations, very few can exist – nor do we cite the ethics chapter with which most textbooks end. Finally, Willihnganz's French is not much better than Ferré's German, so we decided early on to cite sources only if they are in English. The bibliography is therefore a list of every book as well as every article in popular, professional, and academic periodicals on ethics and public relations that we were able to find and summarize. We probably have not found every English-language publication, particularly because professional newsletters appear and disappear often without a single index citation, but we are confident that we have found most of them through 1990.

THEMES

The search yielded nearly three hundred sources on ethics and public relations published since 1922. Four characteristics of these sources as a whole became apparent during the search. First, sparsity: Although public relations is fond of calling itself the conscience of the corporation, relatively few articles and books have been written on the morality of the practice. No more than four were published per year, on average, since 1924. Of course, the sources are spread unevenly; half of them were published during the 1980s. The concern for ethics in public relations has thus paralleled the growth of applied ethics as a field, probably to a large degree in response to the decline in public confidence in institutions in the United States following the Vietnam War and Watergate.

Second, intuition: The publications on ethics and public relations are mostly short, intuitive essays; there are few book-length evaluations of the practice of public relations. This brevity may have eased the bibliographers' task, but it will certainly frustrate the efforts of those who may want to examine PR more systematically and thoroughly. The sources' brevity and intuitive character are indexes to the field's stage of moral development. They may also be indicative of PR's insularity, for even though public relations is involved in every imaginable enterprise, few disinterested observers have studied the field. Those who have written about ethics and public relations have most often made pronouncements about their own experience or about an immediate issue. Their range has been short; their perspective personal.

Third, professionalism: As the table on page 25 illustrates, articles on ethics and public relations have appeared most often in trade publications. Until five years or so ago, few articles had been published in academic journals. This feature correlates with the intuitive nature of the articles, their brevity, and their insularity. Moreover, there is a surprising lack of illustration or case study in these sources; most are platitudinous. Discussions of ethics and public relations are largely absent from broader discussions of the ethics of communication, mass media, or even journalism. Given that most of the sources have been written by and for public relations practitioners, it is no wonder that they tend to be slim, narrowly focused, and hortatory.

Fourth, affirmation: The positive nature of these sources probably reflects the upbeat quality of the practice of public relations. In fact, given that most publications have been written by practitioners and have appeared in trade publications, it would be surprising if the sources were not positive. Regrettably, there is a quality of PR for PR here, which advances the study of public relations little more than kiss-and-tell exposés do. Still, ethics is a hopeful enterprise, so the affirmation in these sources is in keeping with the spirit of moral inquiry. It remains for writers on ethics and public relations to discern the democratic contributions public relations can make without being narrowly self-serving, cliché-ridden, or Pollyannaish.

The works cited in this bibliography articulate a moral principle for all public relations practitioners to follow: always tell the truth. Yet when this maxim is juxtaposed against recent news reports about Anthony Franco's acceptance of the presidency of the Public Relations Society of America while under investigation by the Securities and Exchange Commission, the PRSA Ethics Board's investigation of four members for possible code violations in their meetings with then CIA head William Casey, and general perceptions of PR people as "low-life liars,"[3] one wonders what standard of truth is operating. PR may mean "truth, well told,"[4] but which truth? And who decides?

The works on PR and ethics detailed in this volume follow three lines of inquiry in attempting to answer these questions. One examines the definition of public relations as a source of truth and ethical behavior. Another explores the role and identity of the PR practitioner. A third investigates the nature of truth itself.

McBride points out that much of the confusion about the nature of truth in public relations is imbedded in the history and definition of the practice.[5] Rooted in publicity and press agentry, grandfathered by P. T. Barnum's gleeful belief that "there's a sucker born every minute," and grounded in the economic practicalities of profit-making, contemporary public relations is shackled to an ancestry of shenanigans and shady dealings. Although modern definitions of PR clearly move the field away from these early beginnings, survey results show that cynicism continues. Gitter and Jaspers found that undergraduates learn to trust accountants and social workers, but to distrust salespeople and PR practitioners.[6] Remarks such as the one made by Matt Zachowsky, president of NYCOM Associates, a New York public relations and marketing firm, that "if Col. North is lying he's lying very well, which would make him a highly excellent PR guy," still abound.[7] When asked to compare their moral standards to those of twenty-five other professions, PR professionals ranked themselves in the lower half.[8] Olasky, perhaps PR's most persistent critic, charges the field with undermining the free enterprise system, ignoring morality, and engaging in behind-the-scenes manipulation against the public interest. His "Scam Awards" illustrate what he sees as the duplicity of PR.[9] McCann's exposé of PR at United Fruit gives numerous examples of how public relations helps "to screw up the world."[10]

This critical voice, however vehement, sounds in a minority of articles, most of which appear in newspapers and periodicals such as the *Wall Street Journal, Advertising Age*, and *Jack O'Dwyer's Newsletter* or in published books. Most of the literature on PR and ethics strongly endorses the field and frequently defines it in terms of its ethical obligations. Bateman, for example, states that PR is more than propaganda because ethical tenets guide PR behavior.[11] For Bernays, PR is not quackery but the "science of public opinion" defined as honest advocacy and the scientific use of principles of persuasion. Others believe that persuasion as such is ethical unless it is used immorally. For Ivy Lee, objectivity and publicity are the key elements. According to Pearson, ethical PR depends on creating mutually satisfying relationships between an organization and its publics.[12] A host of writers asserts that PR is the conscience of the organization, that honest public relations ensures that corporations operate in the public interest.

For the most part, these writings define PR as a field concerned with managing two-way interactions with publics in ways that reflect honesty, trust, and principles of social responsibility. Because PR deals with human beings, and PR activities can be used for good or evil, PR must be guided by justice and good character.

Another question many of these writings address involves the source of such moral principles. Because PR borrows heavily from other fields, calls for the application of ethical principles developed elsewhere are not surprising. Bateman urges PR to look to philosophy for a structure that can serve as the source of its ethics.[13] Fairman suggests that St. Bernadine, an Italian monk known for his communication skill, be established as the patron saint of PR.[14] Prout argues that business ethics should not be held as a model for PR, because economic language is ill suited to ethical discussions and corporate structures serve to reduce accountability.[15] Bivens fruitfully applies utilitarianism to PR problems.[16] Culbertson encourages PR people to look to behavioral science theory for a moral base, because such understanding can lead practitioners to define their roles in terms of the positive contributions they can make to society.[17]

In one of the most precise statements concerning PR and ethics, Sullivan argues that because value systems underlie moral decision making, different functions of PR underlie different moral issues. PR techniques are measured by efficiency and economy rather than by moral criteria. As such, they are amoral. PR as partisanship is rooted in loyalty, trust, and obedience to the institution being promoted. Although usually praiseworthy, these values can lead to deceit and injustice. Finally, PR can value human rights. As such, one acknowledges the right to true information and the right to participate in decisions concerning all matters of personal relevance. Here PR finds its true raison d'être, for only this function assures free discussion of true information as a matter of respect.[18]

PR can also look to its practitioners as a source of its morality. Those taking this position argue that ethical PR is based on individual responsibility, with the virtuous public relations practitioner making individual appraisals and arriving at individual judgments. Contending that the field of PR is as moral as those who practice in it, several authors investigated the morality or ethical principles of PR people themselves. Wright's survey of PR practitioners found that most of them exhibited a "moderate to high" level of social responsibility. Many indicated that they would be more professional and socially responsible if their jobs would allow them to do so.[19] Ryan and Martinson interviewed PR practitioners and found that most were guided by ethical relativism, which caused them great stress.[20] Cort likened PR people to parsons: they are not flacks and liars but "unpretentious, friendly, unspectacular people."[21] Bivens distinguished between PR people in terms of their roles as advocates or counselors. He argued that advocates or technicians, because they are employees of an organization, must serve the employer's purpose. Counselors or advisers can serve the client, society, and the profession because they are autonomous agents who defer to professional codes of ethics when faced with moral dilemmas. Although both counselors and advisers must make moral decisions, advisers are in a position to reduce role conflict and make stronger ethical arguments.[22]

If, as these studies indicate, PR people are about as moral as anyone else, why are they still labeled "high-paid errand boys and buffers for management," "hucksters," or "impotent, evasive, egomaniacal and lying"?[23] Why could Nixon urge, "Let's PR it," in response to notification of the Watergate break-in? Why did Olasky's interviews with fifty PR people show that most of them saw hiding the truth as part of "an honest day's work"?

One answer to these questions is that what constitutes truth in PR is objective, consensual, or interpretive. Whether something is true is mitigated by the intent behind telling the truth and the extent to which part or all of the truth must be told. Given these alternate views on what constitutes truth itself, it is little wonder that confusion, both within and outside the field, exists.

Proponents of the objectivity position argue that truth exists out there somewhere, and PR people, like everyone else, are obligated to find and disseminate it. This model of truth-telling resembles the traditional ideal of journalism, an understandable parallel, given that news rooms and journalism schools are traditional training grounds for public relations practitioners. Ivy Lee advocated this position, although he was not above creating the events that he could then argue were true. Olasky is another major proponent of this view. He criticizes "amoral" PR practices such as lying to the press and argues that PR must stop catering to the whims of public opinion and either tell the truth or tell people when information is none of their business.[24] Opponents to Olasky's position argue that if organizational policies are good, there is no reason not to tell the whole truth because publics are rational and can make reasoned decisions. Dealing with images is unnecessary, they contend, because the truth will lead to favorable public opinion.

McBride argues that public relations is often unable to abide by the definition of truth as honest, objective disclosure because this concept does not allow for advocacy.[25] A variation on truth-as-objectivity, then, acknowledges that telling the whole truth is sometimes not in the public's or the corporation's best interest. As long as one does not lie, it is permissible to tell half-truths or keep secrets. One of the PR practitioners Olasky interviewed said, "I don't lie. I've never lied. There's a fine line sometimes, but I've never had data in front of me and read off the wrong numbers to a reporter."[26]

The position that truth is objective reality concerns itself with the factuality and comprehensiveness of disclosure. But as Bateman notes, truth involves the intent and effect of a message as well as its content. The selective release of information may be ethical because full, immediate disclosure might cause great harm. Furthermore, because standards for truth-telling change with time and situation, PR people have to adapt to these changes in their quest for truth.[27] For these reasons, most of the writers on PR and ethics argue that truth is interpreted, that meaning lies not in an event but in the interpretation of an event. As such, many truths can be discovered. The job of public relations is to help people choose from among the possible interpretations the one that will be most beneficial to all. The truth, then, can be found in the intentions that guide and the results that are accomplished through advocacy of preferred interpretations.

PR giant Edward Bernays is the best known proponent of this view. He saw no harm in leading people to a desirable place. To increase the sale of pianos, for example, Bernays would not simply urge people to buy them. Instead, he would try to create widespread desire for a music room in the home. He would hire famous decorators to develop an exhibit of music rooms and invite the media and notables from the music world to the exhibition for publicity purposes. Soon people would begin to long for such a room in their own homes. A piano would be a staple in a music room, and the customer, unaware that the desire was unoriginal, would say to a retailer, "Please sell me a piano."[28]

Even with honorable intentions and beneficent results, such "guidance" can be seen as manipulative. It assumes that the PR person can both see what is best for everyone and act on that. Additionally, within the view of interpreted truth, image and reality become inextricably interwoven. What the organization has done pales in relation to what the organization can convince its publics it has or has not done. The created truth becomes the reality; the image is all. Memories of the PR activities of Hitler, Jim Jones, or Jim and Tammy Bakker remind us all too easily of how this position can be used for harm as well as for good, and few adults would appreciate being managed without prior consent, regardless of the outcome.

A third definition of truth is consensus. Truth in this view is neither objective nor interpreted, but agreed upon by the parties involved. As Bateman argued in 1958, credibility comes not from truth but from fulfilling responsibilities to an audience.[29] Grunig's two-way symmetrical model of public relations is based on the ideal of consensus. According to Grunig, different models of PR hold different criteria for truth-telling. Only the two-way symmetrical model acknowledges that mutual understanding is the ultimate goal of PR.[30] Pearson argues that both corporations and publics use communication rules. Understanding these rules, and examining how satisfied parties are with them, can help PR people avoid ethical relativism by focusing attention on how communication can create mutual understanding between publics. According to this view, ethical behavior results from negotiations between organizations and their publics for mutually satisfying agreements.[31]

Attempts to reach mutual understanding have spawned new approaches to PR – such as issues management, public values monitoring, and social responsibility programs – that propose to foster a desired identity for the corporation and help the corporation understand and better serve its publics. Consensus implies consent, and much contemporary public relations involves discovering the public's values and moral standards so that corporate policies and programs can be designed to accommodate them.

This literature reveals a field still struggling to define standards of ethical behavior for itself. Although it may not yet have reached agreement about what it is, who practices it, or how truth should be defined, it has taken measures to ensure that some matrix of ethical standards is practiced.

Following the debates over the nature of truth-telling in public relations is the question of how PR can best institute principles of truth-telling corporately and individually. Underlying this question is the drive toward professionalism. The definition of "professional" itself is fuzzy, but most people agree that professionals are those who put the good of society above personal gain, are guided by an enforceable code of ethics, agree upon a common body of knowledge, and support a formal education and accreditation program. Four lines of argument about professionalization can be found in the books and articles cited in this bibliography. Authors debate whether PR is a profession; they discuss the development and enforcement of the Code for Professional Standards for the Practice of PR and its role in encouraging ethical behavior; they question how to restrict who can enter the PR field and call themselves PR counselors; and they examine educational trends to evaluate how well PR is training new practitioners.

PR is sometimes viewed as a profession, sometimes as a trade, and sometimes as an emerging profession. Arguments for conferring professional status to the field suggest that PR people, like lawyers or physicians, desire to serve society to the best of their abilities. PR is seen as a profession by those who acknowledge that it uses special knowledge, tools, and techniques to support positions and leaders who are working to better the lot of humankind, and that it teaches clients and the public to think in terms of the public interest. Bernays, perhaps the most vocal supporter of professional status, argues that because PR has the legitimate purpose of advocacy, it fills an important social function. Although many writers defend PR's professional status, most simply assume it and make offhand references to the "profession of PR" or the "PR professional."

Others strongly argue that PR is not, and never will be, a profession. In *Life in the Crystal Palace*, Harrington asserts that PR can never be a profession like law or medicine because its foundation is fluid.[32] Law and medicine serve justice and humanity, but PR is advocacy for hire that tampers with the truth for the benefit of a client's image. Similarly, Delattre argues that only law, medicine, religion, and education are bona fide professions because they serve interests crucial to human life; however, to the extent that they demonstrate personal integrity, PR practitioners may be said to be acting professionally.[33] Young says that PR is a business practiced with professional standards, not a profession as such, so it should liken itself to accountants rather than lawyers.[34] Taking a slightly different line of argument, Wright points out that because PR is a unique enterprise, debates about its professionalism cannot be resolved; one can assess only the professional orientations toward social responsibility that individual PR practitioners exhibit.[35]

Bridging these two extreme positions are those who identify PR as an emerging profession. According to Harlow, PR practitioners are heterogeneous in their knowledge and community orientation, share inadequacies that marked other emerging professions, have a code of ethics that is too vague to apply to concrete cases, have professional associations for purposes of identity and power, identify standards of professional behavior with the caveat of a grandfather clause, tie credentials to university education, and try to persuade the public of the field's professionalism.[36] Hill praises PR for making great strides toward achieving the status of a profession, but notes that it is still marred by unethical practices and that anyone can claim to be a PR expert.[37] Moss argues that if PR is to grow as a profession, ethical standards must be clarified and professional conduct must be achieved in daily practice.[38]

Whether public relations has actually become a profession, the call and momentum to make it one clearly exist. In their struggle for establishing PR's legitimacy, proponents have campaigned tirelessly for a code, for accreditation standards, and for university credentials.

Developing a strong code of ethics is seen as a cornerstone for professionalization, and dozens of articles deal with this issue. As these writings are examined historically, one can see calls for a code, the development of a code, calls for ways to strengthen and enforce the code, criticisms of the code, violations of the code, and modification and strengthening of the code. Nearly forty of the articles annotated here deal directly with these issues. Shortly after PRSA was formed in 1948, the society adopted the first Code of Professional Standards. Since then the code has remained largely intact, with only minor revisions to strengthen, clarify, and add enforcement mechanisms. Most discussions of the code appear in PRSA's *Public Relations Journal*. They serve to make PRSA members aware of the code, help them understand the role of the Grievance Board and judicial panels, and encourage their compliance with the association's standards. Sometimes explicit, usually implicit, is the premise that the existence of the code ensures professional behavior. So Matrat extols codes (in this case, the Code of Athens adopted by the International Public Relations Association) that protect the sacredness of the human person by regulating the behavior which one human being should adopt toward another.[39] Carey contends that codes inspire public confidence because they indicate that adherents place service ahead of personal gain.[40] Dowd claims that upholding code standards will counter the pejorative use of the term "public relations."[41]

Many of these writers evoke the code as the answer to all questions about PR and ethics. How do we know PR people are behaving ethically? Because we have a code. Can we trust PR? Yes, we have a code. Is PR acting for the good of the society? Yes, the code says we must. Can we trust PR people? Only if they are members of PRSA, who are bound by the code.

No code can do all of this, of course. Even the most comprehensive code of ethics cannot cover all situations. Jurgensen and Lukaszewski suggest that ethical thought must delve below codes of ethics to find foundational principles that can be used to ground moral decision making.[42] Warmer argues that existing codes reflect a need for status rather than essential integrity,[43] and Mechling attacks not only PR people but lawyers and accountants as well, for using codes as shields to protect a group from public review.[44] Others argue that although they look good on paper, codes are seldom enforced. Olasky points out that during the 1970s, PRSA panels tried only four code violations, and only one penalty was incurred. According to Olasky, "One would conclude that only one of the then 10,000 PRSA members did anything wrong during that decade, and his sin was taking business from a fellow PRSA member." He concludes that "the Code of Professional Standards was partly a public relations device to allow claims of adherence to virtue, and partly a matter of constraining free competition."[45] Interestingly, the section of the code forbidding encroachment on another's business was repealed when the Federal Trade Commission Bureau of Competition threatened antitrust action against the PRSA.

The issue of enforcement has been a thorn in the side of the code almost since its adoption. Almost immediately following its passage, there were calls for strengthening it and developing mechanisms to enforce it. Those mechanisms are still weak. Although some writers attempt to counter the perception of weak code enforcement by describing how the grievance board operates, what kinds of violations have been considered, and how the board makes decisions, their attempts are dwarfed by negative news coverage surrounding two recent cases. First is the case of Anthony Franco, who resigned his PRSA membership the day he was to be investigated by the board for alleged violations of SEC regulations. More recently, the board exonerated four PRSA members of advising then CIA director William Casey on strategies to win public support for Latin American policies. After Summer Harrison, who lodged the complaint, disagreed publicly with the board's decision, debates ensued over Article 14 of the code, which states that a member cannot act in ways that might harm another member. The issue in code enforcement over private deliberations for judgments of code violations (a person is innocent until proven guilty) and forthright publicity for all PRSA activities (honest PR requires confession as well as fanfare) has yet to be resolved.

In addition to support for a hearty Code of Professional Standards, the path to professionalism is also marked by calls for licensing or accreditation of PR professionals. Underlying these calls is what Olasky calls the "doctrine of selective depravity." He argues that public relations attempts to excuse its low status by arguing that most PR people are professional and by blaming the "immoral outsiders" for causing trouble. PR's "indifferent reputation is due to the incompetence and dishonesty of a minority of their number – the lunatic fringe of the profession, the headline wheedlers, the something-for-nothing boys, to the antics of the quacks and charlatans who cling to the fringe of our profession, to the snide, weasel-minded, smart, conscienceless lads."[46] Unlike doctors or lawyers who must pass state exams to be certified and allowed to practice, anyone with a telephone and a typewriter can practice public relations.

Despite charges that the problem is with the insiders, not the outsiders, many writers believe that certification would bring public relations one step closer to professionalism by ensuring that the quacks and flacks who sully PR can be distinguished from those who exemplify standards. The current accreditation program does allow those who pass the test to use the initials APR, but the program is voluntary. Nevertheless, supporters of accreditation believe that it ensures that information will be channeled through people who uphold the highest ideals of professionalism and responsibility. Accreditation also establishes the PR professional as a necessary auditor of information and hinders nonaccredited persons from engaging in major PR activities.

While accepting accreditation as a positive step, several writers argue that stronger restrictions are needed. For more than fifty years Bernays has urged the field to require state licensing and registration for PR professionals, and Schuyler calls for licensing tests that would assess judgment as well as technique.[47] Compulsory accreditation, or licensing, raises strong objections based on the First Amendment, however, so state licensing for public relations receives relatively little support.

Finally, because professionals undergo specialized education, several writers examine issues in the education of PR practitioners, especially in terms of ethics. The typical approach is to examine how introductory PR textbooks discuss ethical issues. Culbertson found that all of them posit honesty as a universal principle and excuse misimpressions more frequently than factual inaccuracies.[48] Pratt and Rentner found that all texts identified ethics as an individual choice, and that only *Managing Public Relations* by Grunig and Hunt integrated PR and ethical theory.[49] According to Bivins, the textbooks are shortchanging students who need a conceptual framework from which to study PR ethics.[50]

Ultimately, defining PR as a profession will require establishing that it is essential for the good of society. An enormous amount of energy, paper, and ink has been expended in making the argument that the central moral concern for ethical PR is honesty. One approach discusses the prima facie importance of truth-telling. Another argues that because of PR's enormous influence – it can support democratic community, set community and corporate agendas, and prevent social chaos – ethical grounding is

14

paramount. A third approach values truth because honesty can increase corporate profits.

At least in part, truth is important to society because lies are so harmful. In *Lying*, Sissela Bok outlines the social costs of lies. She says:

> Liars usually weigh only the immediate harm to others from the lie against the benefits they want to achieve. The flaw in such an outlook is that it ignores or underestimates two additional kinds of harm – the harm that lying does to the liars themselves and the harm done to the general level of trust and social cooperation. Both are cumulative; both are hard to reverse.[51]

One reason to tell the truth, then, is that honesty is the fabric from which trust and society is woven. Without trust, a democratic society cannot function. Wise decision making by the people cannot be made without full, accurate information. As much as PR has contributed to an aura of cynicism, cluttered the channels of communication, and distorted truth, it has made substantial contributions to the flow of useful, honest information in our complex society. At its best, PR functions as a libertarian safety valve, ensuring that multiple voices are represented in the court of public opinion. Access to complete, accurate information and participation in relevant decisions are fundamental to democratic decision making. PR bolsters democracy also by helping leaders be concerned for truth and by helping the press report fully and accurately on matters of public importance.[52]

One reason that public relations has become such an important source of information is the press's lack of sufficient personnel and expertise to cover all important issues. PR's role in the dissemination of information leads Jeff and Marie Blyskal to worry that PR controls much of the public agenda. They argue that about half of the content of newspapers is instigated by public relations efforts.[53] PR's ability to monopolize news space, to get for free what ought to be paid advertising, has been criticized for generations. A 1929 article in *Editor & Publisher* included the following:

Eddie Bernays frames it up.
Frames what up?
Frames "news" up.
Eddie Bernays frames "news" up.
And makes the papers cover.

Eddie Bernays gets the cash.
Gets much cash?
Yes, much cash.
Eddie Bernays gets large cash.
That once went into paid space.[54]

PR creates and influences news usually to sell an idea, product, or person, not for the purpose of democratic enlightenment.

The Blyskals and others worry also about the latest version of the press release: VNRs or video news releases. Until the 1970s, public relations practitioners relied upon printed press releases to influence published and broadcast news. Their success was well documented; not only did press releases supply much of the information that news agencies issued, but they also helped determine how news stories were presented.[55] By the mid-1970s, satellite and videocassette technologies had become inexpensive enough for PR practitioners to augment their printed releases with VNRs. Since then, public relations practitioners have used VNRs to promote products or technologies, to assist corporations in crisis, and to publicize corporate announcements.[56]

VNRs have proliferated because organizations perceive them as a cost-effective means to promote products and corporate images. The production and distribution costs for a VNR range from $8,000 for satellite distribution to at least $30,000 for videocassette distribution, making VNRs much less expensive than advertisements.[57] They are also more credible, because by appearing as part of a news broadcast, they receive the coveted third-party endorsement. According to Margie Goldsmith of MG Productions, "My clients come to me and say, 'How can I get free air time?' I tell them about VNRs."[58]

Some VNRs have achieved impressive exposure: 170 television stations used MGM/UA's VNR promoting *WarGames*,[59] 80 million viewers saw Drexel Burnham Lambert's VNR concerning its agreement with the U.S. Attorney's office about junk-bond king Michael Milken,[60] and Starkist's "dolphin-safe" tuna VNR reached 81.2 million viewers.[61] Video news releases are tailored to broadcast and cable news programming, often with former reporters doing the stand-up or with the questions provided so that local anchors can appear to be hosting live interviews. Promotional VNRs often appear in news broadcasts without attribution – the fault, according to PR agencies, of broadcast journalists, not PR practitioners – so that they appear to viewers as news stories generated by reporters. In light of the importance of television to the dissemination of daily news, VNRs are a technological convenience that can slant news to a corporate perspective, setting the agenda and unsettling the watchdog function of the news media.

PR has influenced the corporate agenda as well as the public agenda. Several writers argue that PR efforts have led more corporations to act ethically, to concern themselves with social issues, and to assume more responsibility for the effects of their policies and decisions. Issues management activities, for example, frequently are initiated by a desire to integrate corporate policies and programs with the public interest.[62] Public relations helps clarify the company's role in society and guides the social changes that new technologies help cause.[63] Because PR people act as the conscience of the corporation and are responsible to a morality higher than management authority, they are often the corporate advocates for socially responsible programs and activities.[64] Bernays goes so far as to argue that public relations is "the modern instrument by which [corporations] can fight for productive ends and help to bring order out of chaos."[65] According to Bernays, PR is the "engineering of consent" for the public good. As such, PR people are public servants, protecting us from ourselves.

As Center argues, ethical PR activity could reverse societal instincts toward greed, vanity, and waste.[66] Similarly, if PR can shed its identification with advocacy and persuasion, it can serve to restore and maintain community. After all, PR emerged because of consumerism and the loss of community resulting from new means of communication. PR can help correct these losses by defining communication as doing something with rather than something to publics, by helping organizations and community members become aware of common interests, and by leading their organizations in charitable works.[67]

In a narrower vein, other advocates of honest public relations argue that ethical practices can increase profits. Pollock surveyed six hundred PR professionals and found that 85 percent of them believed that ethical behavior contributes to corporate profits.[68] Examples of how, through full, honest disclosure, Tylenol recovered 90 percent of its previous sales volume despite the deaths of several persons from ingesting adulterated capsules, or how Nestlé's decision to stop promoting infant formula to third-world mothers increased public respect, further support this claim.

There is a dark side to these arguments, which is also articulated in the literature we reviewed. Exposés of the field suggest that the reality of PR falls far short of the ideal. According to Ross, PR hides under the aegis of public interest, when its real purpose is to sell the merits of a corporation and contemporary capitalism.[69] McCann observed so many example of dishonesty and impropriety that he was led to conclude that "public relations was helping to screw up the world. In back of almost every bad situation, every lie, every injustice, I could see the hand of the PR man pulling the strings, making things happen, covering things up. Public relations had taken over the government, the prisons, the protest movement, even the ecology."[70] Among Olasky's illustrations of PR's dishonesty, manipulativeness, domination, and restraint of trade is the report of a chemical company, which cooperated with the union to divert a newspaper reporter who was on to a story about high cancer rates among employees.[71]

Cooney raises the issue of which client to serve in his discussion of PR agents who are harassed by bomb scares, letters, and intimidating phone calls for conducting campaigns on behalf of countries accused of human rights violations.[72] Similarly, Bernstein suggests that supplying PR services to apartheid South Africa poses a moral problem for PR firms. He doubts that everyone is entitled to PR services.[73] One could argue, in a libertarian vein, that every viewpoint should be articulated publicly so that the truth can emerge and be believed fervently. Perhaps in the case of South Africa, PR counsel can help corporations strengthen the South African economy and encourage peaceful change. One might, however, argue just as strongly that pernicious, socially despicable parties should be denounced rather than promoted. The issues of client choice and whose version of reality should be defended are far from being resolved.

Like the boy in Bonhoeffer's illustration who was asked to admit embarrassing information about his family life, public relations exists in a thicket of questions involving truth-telling. What information is legitimate for public review? When is full disclosure appropriate? How should information circulate in a democratic society? What is the meaning of information management: who should be responsible, according to what principles, and on whose behalf? Public relations continues to wrestle with the question Bonhoeffer asked: what is meant by telling the truth? We hope that the following citations will lead to greater conscientiousness and clarity among those who study, teach, and practice public relations, and we hope that they will honor their moral convictions with the same courage with which Bonhoeffer honored his.

NOTES

1. Dietrich Bonhoeffer, *Ethics*, ed. Eberhard Bethge (New York: Macmillan, 1955), 367-68.

2. Clifford Christians and Vernon Jensen, *Two Bibliographies on Ethics* (Minneapolis: Silha Center for the Study of Media Ethics and Law, 1988); Thomas W. Cooper, *Television & Ethics: A Bibliography* (Boston: G.K. Hall & Co., 1988).

3. Marvin N. Olasky, "The Aborted Debate within Public Relations: An Approach through Kuhn's Paradigm," in *Public Relations Research Annual* 1, ed. James E. Grunig and Larissa A. Grunig (Hillsdale, N.J.: Earlbaum Associates, 1989), 87.

4. Donald L. Jensen, "Just What Is a PR Man, Anyway?" *Advanced Management* 24 (May 1959): 12.

5. Genevieve McBride, "Ethical Thought in Public Relations History: Seeking a Relevant Perspective," *Journal of Mass Media Ethics* 4, no. 1 (1989): 5-20.

6. A. George Gitter and Engelina Jaspers, "Are PR Counselors Trusted Professionals?" *Public Relations Quarterly* 27 (Winter 1982): 28-30.

7. Dwayne Summar, "Lying Is Professional Suicide," *Wall Street Journal*, 30 July 1987, 23.

8. Larry R. Judd, "Credibility, Public Relations and Social Responsibility," *Public Relations Review* 15 (Summer 1989): 34-39.

9. Marvin N. Olasky, "The 1984 Public Relations Scam Awards," *Business and Society Review*, Fall 1984, 42-46; Marvin N. Olasky, "The Public Relations Scams of 1985," *Business and Society Review*, Winter 1986, 52-55.

10. Thomas P. McCann, *An American Company: The Tragedy of United Fruit* (New York: Crown, 1976), 152.

11. J. Carroll Bateman, "In Search of Morality," *Public Relations Quarterly* 8 (July 1963): 26-30.

12. Ron Pearson, "Beyond Ethical Relativism in Public Relations: Coorientation, Rules, and the Idea of Communication Symmetry," in *Public Relations Research Annual* 1, ed. James E. Grunig and Larissa A. Grunig (Hillsdale, N.J.: Erlbaum Associates, 1989), 67-86.

13. J. Carroll Bateman, "The Path to Professionalism," *Public Relations Journal* 13 (March 1957): 6-8, 19.

14. Milton Fairman, "A Saint for Madison Avenue," *Public Relations Journal* 17 (November 1961): 14-16.

15. Gerald Prout, "On Expecting Corporate Ethical Reform," *Public Relations Review* 4 (Summer 1978): 13-21.

16. Thomas H. Bivins, "Applying Ethical Theory to Public Relations," *Journal of Business Ethics* 6 (April 1987): 195-200.

17. Hugh M. Culbertson, "Public Relations Ethics: A New Look," *Public Relations Quarterly* 17 (Winter 1973): 15-17, 23-25.

18. Albert J. Sullivan, "Values of Public Relations," in *Information, Influence, & Communication: A Reader in Public Relations*, ed. Otto Lerginger and Albert J. Sullivan (New York: Basic Books, 1965), 412-39.

19. Donald K. Wright, "Analysis of Ethical Principles among Canadian Public Relations Practitioners," *IPRA Review* 9 (May 1985): 23-29.

20. Michael Ryan and David L. Martinson, "Ethical Values, the Flow of Journalistic Information and Public Relations Persons," *Journalism Quarterly* 61 (Spring 1984): 27-34.

21. David Cort, "An Angle on Some 'Squares,'" *The Nation*, 7 December 1957, 424-27.

22. Thomas H. Bivins, "Ethical Implications of the Relationship of Purpose to Role and Function in Public Relations," *Journal of Business Ethics* 8 (January 1989): 65-73.

23. Olasky, "The Aborted Debate within Public Relations," 87.

24. Marvin N. Olasky, "Inside the Amoral World of Public Relations: Truth Molded for Corporate Gain," *Business and Society Review,* Winter 1985, 41-44.

25. McBride,"Ethical Thought in Public Relations History."

26. Marvin N. Olasky, *Corporate Public Relations: A New Historical Perspective* (Hillsdale, N.J.: Lawrence Erlbaum Associates, 1987), 129.

27. J. Carroll Bateman, "A New Moral Dimension for Communication," *Public Relations Journal* 14 (August 1958): 16-17.

28. Olasky, *Corporate Public Relations,* 167.

29. Bateman, "A New Moral Dimension for Communication."

30. James E. Grunig and Todd Hunt, *Managing Public Relations* (New York: Holt, Rinehart and Winston, 1984).

31. Ron Pearson, "Beyond Ethical Relativism in Public Relations: Coorientation, Rules, and the Idea of Communication Symmetry," in *Public Relations Research Annual* 1, ed. James E. Grunig and Larissa A. Grunig (Hillsdale, N.J.: Erlbaum Associates, 1989), 67-86.

32. Alan Harrington, *Life in the Crystal Palace* (New York: Alfred A. Knopf, 1959).

33. Edwin J. Delattre, "Ethics in the Information Age," *Public Relations Journal* 40 (June 1984): 12-15.

34. Davis Young, "We Are in the Business of Enhancing Trust," *Public Relations Journal* 42 (January 1986): 7-8.

35. Donald K. Wright, "Professionalism and Social Responsibility in Public Relations," *Public Relations Review* 5 (Fall 1979): 20-33.

36. Rex F. Harlow, "Is Public Relations a Profession?" *Public Relations Quarterly* 14 (Winter 1970): 37.

37. John W. Hill, "The Future of Public Relations," *Public Relations Journal* 21 (September 1965): 10-13.

38. Edward K. Moss, "Is Public Relations a Profession?" *Public Relations Journal* 6 (October 1950): 7-8, 10.

39. Lucien Matrat, "Ethics and Doubts," *IPRA Review* 10 (November 1986): 17-20.

40. John L. Carey, "Professional Ethics Are a Helpful Tool," *Public Relations Journal* 13 (March 1957): 7, 14, 18.

41. Paul A. Dowd, "Public Deception as a Definition of Public Relations," *Public Relations Journal* 43 (July 1987): 22.

42. John H. Jurgensen and James Lukaszewski, "Ethics: Content before Conduct," *Public Relations Journal* 44 (March 1988): 47-48.

43. George A. Warmer, "Public Relations and Privacy," in *Information, Influence, & Communication: A Reader in Public Relations*, ed. Otto Lerginger and Albert J. Sullivan (New York: Basic Books, 1965), 440-65.

44. Thomas B. Mechling, "The Mythical Ethics of Law, PR and Accounting," *Business and Society Review,* Winter 1976-77, 6-10.

45. Olasky, *Corporate Public Relations,* 128.

46. "The Aborted Debate within Public Relations," 88, 89.

47. Philip N. Schuyler, "Dean of PR Seeks to Raise Craft Level," *Editor & Publisher*, 27 February 1960, 26.

48. Hugh M. Culbertson, "How Public Relations Textbooks Handle Honesty and Lying," *Public Relations Review* 9 (Summer 1983): 65-73.

49. Catherine A. Pratt and Terry Lynn Rentner, "What's Really Being Taught about Ethical Behavior," *Public Relations Review* 15 (Spring 1989): 53-66.

50. Thomas H. Bivens, "Ethical Implications of the Relationship of Purpose to Role and Function in Public Relations."

51. Sissela Bok, *Lying: Moral Choice in Public and Private Life* (New York: Vintage Books, 1978), 25.

52. R. A. Paget-Cooke, "Public Relations . . . A Bulwark of Democracy," *Public Relations Quarterly* 4 (Fall 1960): 11-15.

53. Jeff Blyskal and Marie Blyskal, *PR: How the Public Relations Industry Writes the News* (New York: William Morrow, 1985).

54. Marlen Pew, "Shop Talk at Thirty," *Editor & Publisher*, 7 December 1929, 54.

55. F. Dennis Hale, "Press Releases vs. Newspaper Coverage of California Supreme Court Decisions," *Journalism Quarterly* 55 (Winter 1978): 696-702.

56. Alissa Rubin, "Video News Releases: Whose News Is It?" *Public Relations Journal* 41 (October 1985): 19.

57. Maureen Shubow Rubin, "VNRs: Re-examining 'Unrestricted Use,'" *Public Relations Journal* 45 (October 1989): 60.

58. Rubin, "Video News Releases," 18.

59. Blyskal and Blyskal, *PR*, 101.

60. "VNR Update: Facts Versus Fiction," *Public Relations Journal* 45 (December 1989): 23.

61. Adam Shell, "VNR Update: An Easy Guide to VNR Suppliers," *Public Relations Journal* 46 (December 1990): 28.

62. Robert L. Heath and Richard Alan Nelson, *Issues Management: Corporate Public Policymaking in an Information Society* (Newbury Park, Calif.: Sage, 1986).

63. Betsy Ann Plank, "The New Technology and Its Implications for the Public Relations Profession," *IPRA Review* 7 (August 1983): 35-38.

64. Michael Ryan and David L. Martinson, "The PR Officer as Corporate Conscience," *Public Relations Quarterly* 28 (Summer 1983): 20-23.

65. Cited in Olasky, *Corporate Public Relations*, 83.

66. Alan H. Center, "Public Relations: The Stubborn Opportunity," *Public Relations Quarterly* 22 (Winter 1977): 5, 7.

67. Dean Krukeberg and Kenneth Starck, *Public Relations and Community: A Reconstructed Theory* (New York: Praeger, 1988).

68. John C. Pollock, "Business Ethics Affect Bottom Line," *Communication World,* July/August 1989, 49.

69. Irwin Ross, *The Image Merchants: The Fabulous World of Public Relations* (Garden City, N.Y.: Doubleday, 1959).

70. McCann, *An American Company*, 152.

71. Marvin N. Olasky, "Chemical Giant Hoodwinks the Press," *Business and Society Review,* Summer 1985, 60-63.

72. John E. Cooney, "Vox Unpopular: Public Relations Firms Draw Fire for Aiding Repressive Countries," *Wall Street Journal,* 31 January 1979, 1, 30.

73. Jack Bernstein, "South Africa: A Thorny Ethics Problem," *Advertising Age,* 18 November 1985, 84, 93.

Acknowledgments

Discovering and actually getting our hands on the following references are tasks for which we have had plenty of help. Barbara Prior, diligent and cheerful reference librarian at the University of Louisville, searched on-line data bases and told us which printed sources would be most useful. Tom Cooper of Emerson College, Amy Goldfarb of the PRSA Information Center, Dean Kruckeberg of the University of Northern Iowa, Susan Rosenberg of Jack Guthrie & Associates, and Maureen Ward of the O'Dwyer Company supplied additional information, leads, and sources. Ljiljana Kuftinec and Judy Herndon of the university's Interlibrary Loan Office found sources promptly, even when we submitted partial or faulty reference information to them. Our work-study student, Diane Clark, spent the better part of a year double-checking, locating, retrieving, and filing sources. Henriette Campagne, editor at G.K. Hall, offered timely advice and service. We are grateful to all of them for their encouragement, cooperation, persistence, intelligence, and good humor.

Periodicals Most Frequently Cited

Periodical	Number of Articles Cited
Public Relations Journal	72
Public Relations Quarterly	28
Public Relations Review	17
Jack O'Dwyer's Newsletter	14
IPRA Review	13
Journal of Mass Media Ethics	11
Editor & Publisher	10
The Wall Street Journal	8
pr reporter	8
O'Dwyer's PR Services Report	7
Business and Society Review	6
Advertising Age	5
Communication World	4
Journal of Business Ethics	4
Journalism Quarterly	4
Harvard Business Review	3
Other periodicals (34)	1 or 2

Public Relations and Ethics

1 Abend, Albert, and Marvin Olasky. "PR Debate." *Business and Society Review* 50 (Summer 1985): 93-94.

Responding to Olasky's criticisms of "amoral" PR practices such as lying to the press, Abend suggests that Olasky is unaware of the different roles PR people and journalists play in the society. There is not one truth, but divergent truths that PR people help clients choose. Journalists know that PR people are expressing a point of view that reflects corporate self-interest and no lying is involved. The code of professional conduct that guides the activities of PR people reflects the moral commitment most members have made to their profession. If people want to understand PR, they should not read Olasky but look to Bernays, Cutlip, and Lesly.

Olasky responds that he would be delighted if readers would turn to Bernays because Bernays was the first to refer to PR as "manipulation." Bernays believed in behind-the-scenes control by PR people and defined the PR person as a "propaganda specialist." Hiding behind the PRSA Code of Professional Standards will not allow an honest debate which acknowledges that most of PR is manipulation. Although many PR people are likable and honest individuals, the problem of PR lies in its ideology, and that is where debate must begin.

2 Adngelo, Jean Marie. "PR Firms Want 'Pay for Play,'" *Folio*, February 1989, 26-27.

Several PR firms in the United States, such as Results Only Communications, charge their clients on the basis of the amount and prestige of information they place in the media rather than on the basis of commissions. Critics believe that this practice debases relations between the media and the PR profession.

3 Agee, William. "The Role of Public Relations." *Public Relations Journal* 34 (September 1978): 53-54.

Since PR involves social awareness, community orientation, and involvement, CEOs appreciate a comprehensive PR program. But there are some disturbing trends in PR. PR people must balance generating publicity for the company and for the CEO. They must stop trying to prove their importance, and stop quibbling about distinctions between PR and related fields such as government relations and civic affairs. In short, PR people need to stop the public debate about PR's need for time, access, and organizational power, and focus more on new communication technologies and strategies. Finally, they need to stop emphasizing the need for honest, candid communication because this stance assumes that the clients do not adhere to the same high standards PR does.

4 Ahlfeld, William J. "Why Decision Makers Must Have a Conscience." *Public Relations Journal* 17 (July 1961): 17-19.

Public relations should be the conscience of the organization rather than a "relay mechanism" through which company policies are broadcast. The public is composed of rational people who are capable of making reasoned decisions. Therefore, if organizational policies are good, public relations results will be favorable. On the other hand, public relations people cannot use persuasion to "change a bad opinion of a poor policy." The long-term harm in "arranging the truth" or "telling half-truths" will be impossible for the company to overcome.

5 Appley, Lawrence A. "The Obligations of a New Profession." *Public Relations Journal* 4 (December 1948): 4-9.

Before public relations can help society understand and adapt to change, it needs to recognize its social responsibilities and obligations. To do this, PR requires an accepted definition, written professional objectives, clarification of practitioner responsibilities and qualifications, establishment of research, apprenticeship and educational programs, development of national awards, and the institution of a professional code of ethics.

6 "Article 14 of the PRSA Code Must Go!" *O'Dwyer's PR Services Report*, August 1989, 4.

Public Relations Society of America (PRSA) member Summer Harrison publicly criticized four members who attended a 1983 meeting with the late William Casey, a member of President Ronald Reagan's cabinet. Some PRSA officers felt that Harrison's action broke article 14 of the PRSA code: "A member shall not intentionally damage the professional reputation or practice of another practitioner." This article violates legal precedent, which allows a member of a profession to criticize publicly any actions that threaten the integrity of that profession. Freedom of speech is guaranteed, regardless of professional affiliation. Further, the PRSA's practice of secretive ethical review is itself questionable, and PRSA should consider dropping it in favor of a more open and modern disciplinary process.

7 Awad, Joseph F. "Putting a Price on Publicity." *Public Relations Journal* 43 (November 1987): 18-20.

The practice of charging PR clients only if stories are placed has at least three ramifications. First, the practice may generate media resentment because most editors and journalists feel indignant about being "delivered." Second, making payment contingent on placement might lead PR people to badger media people and cause further resentment. The third and most serious concern is that this practice focuses on publicity as an end in itself, and as such forces attention away from a comprehensive view of PR. It reflects short-term thinking, and it is unethical to sell publicity and allow clients to think they are getting PR – especially if the publicity is not going to advance their goals.

8 Barovick, Richard L. "Status Report: Code of Conduct for MNCs." *Public Relations Journal* 35 (October 1979): 30-32.

Controversy over multinational corporations (MNCs) has largely subsided because of the success of long-term education campaigns stating the positive effects of MNCs and the successful adoption of codes of conduct that regulate executives' behaviors.

The code of conduct was adopted by the Organization for Economic Cooperation and Development (OECD), a twenty-four-nation organization that coordinates members' policies. Two key code issues are (1) a set of behavioral standards outlining government treatment of foreign companies and (2) a "transparency" agreement, which states that continuing public disclosure is necessary so publics will know and understand what the companies are doing.

The code does not substitute for national laws but is currently the only set of norms that crosses national boundaries. Seventy American companies said they comply almost 100 percent with the code.

9 Bartle, Franklin W. "Tell the People." *Printer's Ink,* 21 February 1964, 68.

Public relations activities designed to make corporations seem like kindly big brothers may do a disservice. Corporations exist to make money, and the economic concerns that drive corporate practice are far removed from what they preach. There is no reason corporate achievements can't be recognized, but "exuding sweet froth" leaves the public unaware that "real wolves sometimes scratch at the doors." When corporations need to cut back on philanthropy or lay workers off, the public feels misled.

10 Bateman, J. Carroll. "A New Moral Dimension for Communication." *Public Relations Journal* 14 (August 1958): 16-17.

As the communications industry continues to grow, the PR practitioner bears the responsibility for developing voluntary ethical controls. Although PR ethics has discussed relationships between clients and practitioners and among practitioners, there has been little examination of the ethics of communication itself. PR people must examine both the denotation and connotation of their words and must be careful that their words are not so adapted or ambiguous that they are misleading. Truth lies not only in the content of a message but also in its intent and result, and PR will be judged accordingly. PR will gain credibility through meeting this responsibility to the audience.

11 Bateman, J. Carroll. "In Search of Morality." *Public Relations Quarterly* 8 (July 1963): 26-30.

Public relations needs to delineate and define the ethical principles that govern decisions, because ethical tenets distinguish the field morally from simple propaganda. Ethical principles governing PR activities must include education, appeals to judgment and reason, truth, belief in the democratic process, willingness to subjugate selfish interests to the interests of society, and respect for the freedom of individuals to make their own decisions.

12 Bateman, J. Carroll. "The Path to Professionalism." *Public Relations Journal* 13 (March 1957): 6-8, 19.

In the fifty years since PR "declared its independence from its shoddy parents – press agentry and ballyhoo," it has made great strides toward professionalism. Like architecture and engineering, PR borrows information from other fields and applies it in concrete situations. Unlike these professions, however, PR deals with human beings, and there is a moral implication to actions.

Before PR can be a full-fledged profession it must develop a philosophic structure to serve as the source of its ethics. Defining PR as persuasion will not lead to this goal. PR practitioners must dedicate themselves to disseminating enlightenment to be truly professional.

13 Bates, Don. "Are Practitioners Lazy When It Comes to Ethics?" *Public Relations Journal* 40 (March 1984): 4-5.

PR should be at the center of the business ethics debate because it is PR's job to design and direct the programs that ensure corporate responsibility. PR is not at the center because of laziness, and this lack of involvement is costly.

PR practitioners should become part of the ethics discussion in corporations where they work and ensure that their actions are responsible to themselves, their publics, and their employers.

14 Battiata, Mary. "Public Relations or 'News': Gray & Co. Blurs Boundaries." *Washington Post,* 28 March 1985, A1, A9.

Video news releases are appearing as part of television news broadcasts. Beamed inexpensively by satellite, they feature former or free-lance TV news reporters. Companies that produce video news releases notify television stations and label their product as public relations, but some broadcasters air them without disclaimer or identification.

15 Bennett, James R. "Corporate Sponsored Image Films." *Journal of Business Ethics* 2, no. 1 (1983): 35-41.

In order to diffuse the power of slick and seductive films produced to enhance corporate images and aims, schools should train students to be methodically skeptical.

16 Bernays, Edward L. "The Case for Licensing and Registration for Public Relations." *Public Relations Quarterly* 24 (Fall 1979): 26-28.

Licensing and registration for public relations practitioners are essential to professionalize the practice. With precedents for licensing extending back to the mid-nineteenth century, public relations need not fear government intervention or restrictions on expression because the government protects people and ensures freedom, nor should public relations worry that licensing would make PR overly restrictive because the profession would be open to all qualified individuals.

17 Bernays, Edward L. "Gaining Professional Status for Public Relations." *Public Relations Quarterly* 25 (August 1980): 20.

State licensing and registration of public relations practitioners are required if PR is to become a profession. The groundwork has been laid: PR has been defined, educational and experiential requirements have been specified, and ethical standards have been outlined.

18 Bernays, Edward L. "Hucksterism vs. Public Relations." *Public Relations Quarterly* 21 (Fall 1976): 16.

Many public relations seminars offered by management and advertising associations emphasize skills and ignore ethics, social responsibility, and public relations principles. Public relations must be defined through state registration and licensing to ensure that professionalism is not replaced by hucksterism.

19 Bernays, Edward L. "The Outlook for Public Relations." *Public Relations Quarterly* 10 (Winter 1966): 34-38.

The role of the public relations practitioner is to serve as an adviser to top-level management on how to win public favor. To do this, public relations must be seen as a profession, its practitioners must be generalists and specialists, and the highest standards of ethics must be upheld.

20 Bernays, Edward L., and Ferdinand Lundberg. "Does Propaganda Menace Democracy? A Debate." *Forum*, June 1938, 341-45.

Freedom of opinion, essential to a democratic society, is accomplished through propaganda. Propaganda attempts to modify people's ideas or behavior by presenting alternative points of view and allowing choices to be made among them. Because most propagandists today are paid advocates, however, their invisibility poses a threat to the truths freedom should guarantee. They will spread any opinion for which they are paid, and this propaganda often reflects the opinions of power-seeking groups. As such, it can do great harm.

21 Bernstein, Jack. "The Deaver Affair–Bad News for Public Relations." *Advertising Age*, 26 May 1986, 76.

Whether or not former Reagan staffer Michael Deaver is guilty of violating conflict-of-interest laws or engaging in other illegal acts, he has violated the spirit of the law by using his continued entrée to the White House to attract PR clients. He has failed to manage the image problems this appearance of manipulation has created, and his actions have repercussions for the whole PR field, because "just a whiff of impropriety casts a pall over the entire process."

22 Bernstein, Jack. "The Franco Fiasco–The Wages of Sin." *Advertising Age*, 27 October 1986, 76.

Anthony Franco resigned as president of PRSA after being accused of using privileged information to buy stock. Although this incident, and the inept way PRSA handled it, garnered enormous negative publicity for public relations, something good may yet come of it. Franco wanted to be a role model for younger members, and "by dramatizing the penalties of engaging in illicit practices, he may have succeeded in making that a reality."

23 Bernstein, Jack. "South Africa: A Thorny Ethics Problem." *Advertising Age*, 18 November 1985, 84, 93.

Supplying PR services for apartheid South Africa poses a thorny ethics problem for PR firms. Although people generally agree that apartheid is wrong, members of some firms argue that South African clients should be served: everyone has a right to PR counsel, and PR activities can help corporations strengthen the South African economy and lay ground for peaceful change. Others, including Bernays and Finn, argue that because PR does not deal with law, but with public opinion and sentiment, not everyone is entitled to PR services. If something is morally wrong, it should not be promoted or defended.

24 Beyers, Bob. "In Public Relations and Fund Raising, Colleges Should Remember: Candor Pays." *Chronicle of Higher Education,* 8 August 1990, B1, B3.

Forthrightness about information, both flattering and embarrassing, can lead to unexpected financial and enrollment gains for colleges.

25 Bissland, James H., and Terry Lynn Rentner. "Education's Role in Professionalizing Public Relations: A Progress Report." *Journal of Mass Media Ethics* 4, no. 1 (1989): 92-105.

PR is striving to become a profession in part by encouraging formal education in public relations. But according to a survey of 650 members of the Public Relations Society of America and the International Association of Business Communications, only 14.8 percent of practitioners have any formal education in public relations (most have studied some facet of communication, however), and those who do are nearly identical to those who do not in terms of their perceptions of autonomy in the workplace, their understanding of the practice of public relations, and their commitment to job and career. Judged according to specialized education, then, public relations is at most a semiprofession.

26 Bivins, Thomas H. "Applying Ethical Theory to Public Relations." *Journal of Business Ethics* 6 (April 1987): 195-200.

Basic ethical theories are rarely applied to public relations relations problems. The ethical theories available depend on the person's public relations role. The communication advocate/technician creates and disseminates information. The communication adviser/manager plans and gives advice. The roles differ in degree of objectivity, responsibility to the client, and most crucially, autonomy.

A public service advertisement comparing the alcohol content of a beer, a glass of wine, and 1.5 oz. of distilled liquor is examined using ethical theories. This examination reveals that the pubic relations adviser role, since it is the only "professional" role, allows the PR person to make stronger ethical arguments without role conflict. First, the adviser can appeal to the PRSA Code of Professional Conduct. Codes may not cover all situations, but articles 6 and 9, pertaining to hidden interests and integrity of communication channels, can be evoked in this case. Additionally, the adviser's professional autonomy allows him or her to point out the immorality of withholding the intent of the advertisement, namely, to increase sales. Finally, the adviser's prima facie duty to the client is outweighed by the obligation to act on behalf of a larger community. Although both advocates and advisers must make ethical decisions, issues of morality are best left to those in positions of authority.

27 Bivins, Thomas H. "Are Public Relations Texts Covering Ethics Adequately?" *Journal of Mass Media Ethics* 4, no. 1 (1989): 39-52.

Teaching PR ethics requires a grounding in basic ethical theory. Ethics coverage in six widely used introductory texts differs in terms of the context in which they discuss PR ethics, as well as the depth, focus, level, and balance of that discussion. Although all of the texts note that the PR practitioner is key to discussion of social responsibility within the organization, no accepted conceptual framework from which to study PR ethics is presented. The texts may be shortchanging students who need deeper insight into ethical decision-making processes if they are to function in a complex moral environment.

28 Bivins, Thomas H. "Ethical Implications of the Relationship of Purpose to Role and Function in Public Relations." *Journal of Business Ethics* 8 (January 1989): 65-73.

Like lawyers, PR professionals have two roles: the advocate and the counselor. The advocate is responsible for serving the employer's purpose; the counselor, by contrast, primarily serves the profession. Unlike the advocate, the counselor plays an active part in determining the client's purpose. Ethical guidelines in public relations should account for the duality in roles, functions, and purposes, as the professional guidelines for lawyers do.

29 Bivins, Thomas H. "Professional Advocacy in Public Relations." *Business and Professional Ethics Journal* 6 (Spring 1987): 82-90.
   Advocacy in public relations is professional when the PR counselor first determines that the client's goals are moral. If they are, the PR counselor can advocate the client's case, taking measures to ensure the morality of both the message and the techniques of dissemination.

30 Bivins, Thomas H. "A Theory-Based Approach to Public Relations Ethics." *Journalism Educator* 45 (Winter 1991): 39-44.
   All students of public relations should be required to take a course in ethics, minimally in media ethics and ideally in the ethics of public relations. Students should study major deontological and teleological theories in terms of the counseling and advocacy functions of public relations and in the context of in-house, agency, and counseling models. Students should also distinguish public relations from journalism and see ethical public relations in light of issues of professionalism and theories of communication.

31 Black, Jay, Dennis Wilcox, Ralph Barney, Stanley Cunningham, and Deni Elliott-Boyle. "A Public Relations Dilemma." *Journal of Mass Media Ethics* 1 (Fall/Winter 1985-86): 78-83.
   Four PR professors discuss solutions to a case involving a PR person who was asked to keep secret the company's decision to close a steel plant. Many people will be adversely affected by this, including the PR person's sister and brother-in-law. All four professors agreed that the PR person cannot disclose information about the decision to her family. Rationales appeal to (1) the PRSA Code of Professional Conduct, article 5; (2) the corporation's obligation to disclose the information to everyone; (3) ethical theories that suggest that the greatest good to the most people will come from silence; and (4) the fact that the company may be keeping silent so it has time to prepare programs to help employees relocate and adjust in the most supportive way.

32 Blyskal, Jeff, and Marie Blyskal. *PR: How the Public Relations Industry Writes the News.* New York: William Morrow and Co., 1985.
   Because it knows how to manipulate the mass media, public relations controls much of the public agenda. The press, lacking

manpower and expertise, relies upon public relations so much that about half of newspaper content is initiated by public relations efforts. PR molds public opinion not so much by lying as by getting the press to endorse the perspectives that PR desires. PR creates and influences news, always with a plug, always with the goal of selling something–an idea, a product, a person. So that the public can receive a disinterested picture of the world, the press needs to wrest control of news content from public relations. To resist PR, the press must live up to its own rhetoric, investigating stories more deeply, carefully, and completely, ignoring media events, and being ever watchful for PR salesmanship.

33 Booth, Alyse Lynn. "Franco Brings Entrepreneurial Drive to PRSA Presidency." *Public Relations Journal* 42 (January 1986): 14.

Through incessant work, Anthony M. Franco built a multimillion-dollar PR firm in Detroit. As PRSA president, he plans to examine professionalism and increase awareness of PRSA's Code of Professional Standards.

34 Brain, John. "Openness–or Irrationality?" *Public Relations Journal* 44 (December 1988): 39-40.

The public expects a company charged with wrongdoing to confess, even though the company may be blameless. Companies often comply by finding a scapegoat.

35 Brown, David H. "A Funny Thing Happened on the Way to the Forum on Ethics." *Public Relations Quarterly* 31 (Spring 1986): 20-23.

Codes of ethics are worthless without hearty enforcement procedures, so they will not advance public relations toward professional status. Certification, along the lines of a stringent master's degree, will. Certification could be administered by a National Academy of Professional Communication, an umbrella organization also responsible for training, research, and publication.

36 Brown, Robert U. "World Congress Endorses Code of Conduct for PR." *Editor & Publisher,* 3 June 1961, 15, 73.

The International Public Relations Association adopted a fifteen-point Code of Conduct.

37 Brown, Thomas L. "Honesty Is the Best (PR) Policy." *Industry Week,* 7 November 1988, 13.

Pete Johnson, head of Johnson Communications Inc. of Phoenix, believes that good public relations means honest advocacy. To support the safety claims of Brahma Topper, a camper inserted into the bed of a pickup truck, Johnson hired a stunt driver to flip a truck equipped with a Brahma Topper at 30 miles per hour two times. A media audience witnessed this successful demonstration and reported the results to a national audience.

38 Brownell, Atherton. "Publicity–And Its Ethics." *North American Review*, February 1922, 188-99.

The new profession of press agentry and publicity has come into existence because the press has failed to live up to its highest ideals. If properly governed and regulated, this new profession will act in the public interest.

39 Budd, John F., Jr. "Corporate Ethics and Credibility." *IPRA Review* 10 (August 1986): 17-20.

Because the current interest in ethics is no fad, businesses need to discuss ethics as much as they discuss technology or manufacturing. Business people need to identify values and standards, codify them, communicate them, and never compromise. Increased credibility will result.

40 Budd, John F., Jr., and Richard E. Cheney, Jr. "Executive Forum." *Public Relations Journal* 45 (May 1989): 38-40.

The Drexel Burnham Lambert/Michael Milken "scandal" and the buyout of RJR Nabisco by Kohlberg Kravis Roberts have ethical implications for PR. According to Cheney, though the RJR deal was legal, it was "a most flagrant instance of selfishness." There is reason to be optimistic, however, because people who have acted illegally or unethically have been caught, and though not perfect, securities laws have "strengths too easily overlooked." Instead of "bewailing the times we live in" people should help through public service actions. Budd notes that CEOs must realize that to the public, perceptions are reality, and act not only legally, but in terms of what people will perceive to be right. They must act from a firm philosophical foundation–the current wisdom of "maximizing shareholder value doesn't hold up under scrutiny." Both the Drexel/Milken case, and the buyout of RJR by KKR exhibit violations of these principles.

41 Burger, Chester. "Ethics in Public Relations." *Public Relations Journal* 38 (December 1982): 13, 16-17.

Too often the public receives distorted information not because of lying but because of omission. After the Three Mile Island, Pennsylvania, nuclear accident, for instance, Friends of the Earth reported a rise of thyroid disease among infants, leaving out the

Pennsylvania Department of Health's conclusion that this increase was unrelated to nuclear contamination. Publicists should inform in a balanced, truthful way, never underestimating the audience's perceptiveness.

42 Calver, Homer N. "Now that We Have a Code." *Public Relations Journal* 7 (February 1951): 3-4, 17.

    The newly adopted PRSA Code of Professional Standards needs to be revised to accommodate issues it does not currently address, and acceptance of the code must be secured. This modification requires that PRSA establish mediation, grievance, or judiciary committees and empower them to deal with complaints and to determine appropriate disciplinary measures.

43 Carey, John L. "Professional Ethics Are a Helpful Tool." *Public Relations Journal* 13 (March 1957): 7, 14, 18.

    As the American Institute of Certified Public Accountants illustrates, codes of ethics are as essential to professionalism as are education and examination. Codes inspire public confidence because they indicate that the adherents place service ahead of personal gain; without such ethical professionalism, the group is merely a business.

44 Carey, John L. "Professionalism Is Good for the Public." *Public Relations Journal* 16 (January 1960): 20-23.

    PR professionals are motivated to seek professional status because it will increase the opportunity for service. This desire to serve society to the full extent of one's ability is the essence of professionalization. To secure this status, a common body of knowledge must be agreed upon, a process of formal accreditation must be instituted, and a specific, enforceable code of ethics must be adopted.

45 Carr, Patrick. "Public Relations Professionalism." *Public Relations Quarterly* 16 (Winter 1971): 6, 32.

    Because information can change attitudes and influence decision making, it requires more responsible management than law or accounting. To ensure that information will be channeled through professional and responsible people, PR must establish a professional accreditation program. Information handled by an accredited professional would guarantee the public of factual information and assure editors that they are receiving legitimate news. It would also establish the PR professional as a necessary "auditor" of information for business, government, and agencies and make it very difficult for nonaccredited persons to engage in major PR activities.

46 "Casey Meeting No Ethics Violation–PRSA." *Jack O'Dwyer's Newsletter,* 19 April 1989, 2.

The PRSA board of ethics ruled that the four PRSA members who met with CIA head William Casey in 1983 did not violate the PRSA Code of Professional Standards and that no further investigation was required. The investigation was sparked by Summerlynne Harrison's eleven-page description of ways in which the meeting violated articles 2, 6, and 14 of the code. These articles direct members to act in accord with the public interest, to refuse to engage in any practice that corrupts the integrity of channels of communication or processes of government, and to sever relations with any organization if such a relationship requires conduct contrary to this code.

The decision indicates PRSA's unwillingness to guide members in deciding what is right and wrong.

47 "Casey Wanted Contras to Hit Cities." *Jack O'Dwyer's Newsletter,* 2 November 1988, 7-8.

The five PR executives who met in 1983 with William Casey agreed that the CIA head wanted help in "educating" the U.S. public on activities in Central America. They acknowledged that they spent the morning brainstorming, went to lunch, and then presented ideas to Casey. They may have been used as fronts, however, in that Casey's real motive may have been to sell escalation of the Nicaraguan conflict to the American public. Ron Watt, head of the ethics committee of the Counselors Academy of PRSA said that he believed that the PR executives were acting in "the best interests of their profession and their country."

48 Center, Allen H. "Public Relations: The Stubborn Opportunity." *Public Relation's Quarterly* 22 (Winter 1977): 5, 7.

Exemplary conduct by PR practitioners could reverse societal instincts toward greed, vanity, and waste. For this to happen, however, PR needs to be identified in terms not only of skills but also of firm moral principles. Moral obligations must be upheld by ensuring that persuasive information serves the best interests of all, not just the best interests of the employer. PR must be proclaimed as a legitimate voice in the resolution of social problems. Finally, professionals have an obligation to give back to society and the field of PR as much as they have been given.

49 Ciervo, Arthur V. "The Poor Image of the Image Makers." *Public Relations Journal* 31 (July 1975): 11-13.

Rather than attributing PR's poor image to quacks and rascals, practitioners need to recognize that they, too, contribute to the problem and begin to take ethics seriously. This includes developing a broad knowledge base and refusing to compromise strong personal convictions.

50 Ciervo, Arthur V. "Truth or Consequences." *Currents,* January 1987, 20-24.

Although PR practitioners in colleges and universities rarely lie, they sometimes evade the truth when questioned about unflattering information. To foster genuine trust with the press, PR practitioners should understand the administration's position on full disclosure, respect the reporter's role as questioner, make ethics integral to the hiring of the PR staff, admit bad news, obey the law, be consistent, understand the issues fully, and get to know reporters.

51 "The Code of Ethics of the International Association of Business Communicators." *Jack O'Dwyer's Newsletter,* 12 July 1989, 8.

Article 14 of the PRSA Code of Professional Standards should be expunged. It says members must not "intentionally damage the professional reputation or practice of another practitioner." Although PR practitioners have the right to critize each other to other professionals in the interest of improving quality, other professional groups such as IABC encourage members to speak out if they see something wrong. PRSA should follow this lead and drop article 14 and the entire secretive judicial process.

52 "Codes of Conduct." *pr reporter,* 13 September 1976, 2-3.

In addition to PRSA's Code of Professional Standards for the Practice of Public Relations, two additional codes exist. The Code of Athens was adopted by the International Public Relations Association. Loosely based on the United Nations charter which emphasizes human dignity and rights, the Code of Athens requires that practitioners act in accordance with strict moral principles and social awareness. The personal credo of J. Carroll Bateman reaffirms the value of democratic freedom and the role of PR in a free market society.

53 Collins, Richard S. "Don't Get It Right–Get It Readable." *Public Relations Quarterly* 17 (Summer 1972): 14-16.

Despite many misleading stories printed by the media, the PR person is still required to maintain an open door policy and to make every effort to satisfy the legitimate information needs of its publics. Like lawyers, PR people are paid advocates, not flacks. PR people must be sure to tell the truth and hope that others will do the same.

54 "Comments on PRSA/CIA/Harrison Ethics Case." *Jack O'Dwyer's Newsletter,* 28 June 1989, 8.

Responses of PRSA members to the PRSA Ethics Board's decision on the CIA/Harrison case ranged from outrage to approval. Some members said the board had done its job and discussion should be dropped; others said this issue should be widely discussed; still others noted that Harrison was bound by confidentiality rules and should stop criticizing.

Two other recent cases raise the issue of whether PRSA members should be allowed to discuss public controversies openly. One of these involved Philip Morris's campaign to fight antismoking rules, the other Anthony Franco's case charging that a member had "injured" his reputation by commenting on the SEC consent decree Franco had signed.

55 Cook, Howard F. "How Chicago Council Aids Press Relations." *The Modern Hospital,* June 1965, 117-18, 168.

The Chicago Hospital Council keeps its Guide to Ethical Hospital Press-TV-Radio Relationships alive and meaningful by hosting an annual dinner for hospital and news media representatives, who receive the guide as well as the updated "Directory of Hospitals and Contact List."

56 Cooney, John E. "Vox Unpopular: Public Relations Firms Draw Fire for Aiding Repressive Countries." *Wall Street Journal,* 31 January 1979, 1, 30.

Many PR firms are coming under fire, both literally and figuratively, because of their involvement with nations accused of human rights violations. Although they are hired to polish the images of countries such as Argentina or Haiti, the firms themselves come to be seen by rebels or groups such as Amnesty International as instruments of repression. PR representatives and firms are often harassed by bomb scares, letters, intimidating phone calls, or picket lines.

Most of the firms admit that they take on government clients because of the lucrative pay but also point out that improving the country's image may discourage further harsh activities, encourage foreign investment in the country, and improve citizens' economic outlook. They also argue that every regime has a right to tell its story.

57 Cort, David. "An Angle on Some 'Squares,'" *The Nation,* 7 December 1957, 424-27.

Contrary to current myths, PR people are "unpretentious, friendly, unspectacular people." They are more akin to parsons than to professionals, craftsmen, or artists in that their central concern is morality.

58 "Crisis in Ethics Faces American Business: Amorality No Longer Tenable in Modern Society." *purview,* a supplement of *pr reporter,* 29 February 1988, 1-2.

To prevent government and public retribution for social irresponsibility, more and more businesses are attending to ethics. Irresponsibility results more often from amorality than from immorality: many businesses have simply ignored the morality of their practices. This deficit is untenable. Those companies with explicit moral prohibitions most often forbid extortion, gifts, kickbacks, conflicts of interest, illegal political payments, and violation of laws in general.

59 Culbertson, Hugh M. "How Public Relations Textbooks Handle Honesty and Lying." *Public Relations Review* 9 (Summer 1983): 65-73.

This content analysis of six public relations textbooks found that they use more negative than positive illustrations, posit honesty as a universal principle, and are more likely to excuse misimpressions than factual inaccuracies.

60 Culbertson, Hugh M. "Public Relations Ethics: A New Look." *Public Relations Quarterly* 17 (Winter 1973): 15-17, 23-25.

In contrast to platitudinous discussions of PR ethics, behavioral science theory can give PR practitioners useful information about such concepts and classes as decision making, pro and con presentation of information, differences between understanding and acceptance, and credibility. Behavioral science understanding can lead practitioners to define their roles in terms of the positive contributions they can make to society, help them find new appeals, and encourage them to remember that messages are means to an end, not ends in themselves.

61 Cutlip, Scott M. "A Re-Examination of Public Relations' Platitudes." *Public Relations Journal* 19 (January 1963): 13-16.

Although PR has created an aura of cynicism, cluttered the channels of communication with pseudoevents and phony phrases that confuse public issues, and sometimes distorted the truth by filling the opinion stream with the "debris of diversion and distortion," honest PR people have made substantial contributions to the flow of useful, honest information in our society. They are largely responsible for improving corporate conduct and sensitivity to public opinion. PR has been used successfully to promote many socially beneficial organizations and programs. PR has taken on an enormous responsibility and should move toward professionalization to ensure that the public receives honest, reliable information on which to base sound judgments.

62 Cutlip, Scott M. "Third of Newspapers' Content PR-Inspired." *Editor & Publisher,* 26 May 1962, 68.

Substantial newspaper content is generated by public relations practitioners because newspapers are understaffed, particularly in the areas of business, science, health, religion, art, music, education, and social welfare and because newspapers are too willing to swap space for favors, what Cutlip calls "handout reporting." The press needs to evaluate how well it provides the citizenry with accurate, complete reporting.

63 Decker, Francis K. "The Path towards Professionalism: PRSA's Code and How It Operates." *Public Relations Journal* 19 (April 1963): 7-8.

Built into PRSA's Code of Professional Standards are provisions for its enforcement. The basic requirement for enforcement is the idea that before any disciplinary action may be taken, the member must be advised of the charges against him and be given an opportunity to be heard. Three judicial bodies compose the enforcement network for the code. The National Judicial Council is composed of panels of six members. Each of the ten judicial districts has a panel. The district panels receive complaints relative to code violations, gather information, hold hearings, and make recommendations to the Board of Directors. The Board of Directors reviews this evidence and makes final disciplinary decisions to censure, suspend, expel, or exonerate. A third body, the Grievance Board, was created to watch for violations where no member of the society is directly aggrieved, but society at large has been harmed. All proceedings are confidential and held in closed session.

64 Decker, Francis K. "PRSA's Code: How the Practitioner and Public Are Protected." *Public Relations Journal* 23 (March 1967): 26-29.

Enforcement of the PRSA Code of Professional Standards rests on the code itself, the by-laws of PRSA, and the rules of procedures governing panels adopted by the Board of Directors. Supplementing the code are the board's interpretations. Because the PRSA by-laws stipulate that all proceedings of the three major code enforcement bodies – the National Judicial Council, the Board of Directors and the Grievance Board – are confidential and in closed session, the membership at large sees only the result of this process, and then only when disciplinary measures are taken. For this reason, the members of the society cannot be fully aware of how the code protects them and the public from the results of improper and illegal practices.

65 Delattre, Edwin J. "Ethics in the Information Age." *Public Relations Journal* 40 (June 1984): 12-15.

PR is not a profession per se – only law, medicine, religion, and education are because they serve interests crucial to human beings. However, PR practitioners act professionally to the extent that they demonstrate personal integrity. Clarity in communication is no panacea, because it highlights disagreement and discord at least as often as it leads to understanding and reconciliation. Instead, integrity is the key to addressing the timeless issues that emerging communications technologies present in new forms.

66 "The Demand of Media for 'Exclusives' and PR's Acquiescence in This." *Jack O'Dwyer's Newsletter,* 15 March 1989, 8.

"Exclusives" can lead to difficulty for both media and public relations. Because of an exclusive agreement with the CBS program "60 Minutes," the Natural Resources Defense Council (NRDC) attempted to delay other media from reporting that the use of pesticides on fruits and vegetables was harmful to children. These attempts so angered other media representatives that some of them did not cover a NRDC news conference on the topic. Realizing that the exclusive agreement was causing negative publicity, the NRDC began to talk to other media, which in turn created difficulty with CBS.

67 Dilenschneider, Robert L. *Power and Influence: Mastering the Art of Persuasion.* New York: Prentice Hall Press, 1990.

Good public relations is based on quality and accountability, characteristics that management must establish, exemplify, communicate, and enforce. Marathon Oil's successful escape from Mobil Oil's takeover attempt and the swift and humane handling of Kansas City Hyatt Hotel's disaster both illustrate that managers must be shrewd and forthright in order to achieve business goals and to avoid business losses. Ethics benefits corporations.

68 "Do Job – Don't Talk about It – Ron Watt." *Jack O'Dwyer's Newsletter,* 16 November 1988, 2.

When facing an ethical question, PR people should listen to others, but ultimately they have to make their own judgments about what is proper. Professionals candidly advise their clients and get the job done, but amateurs continually exaggerate how great the job will be.

69 Dowd, Paul A. "Public Deception as a Definition of Public Relations." *Public Relations Journal* 43 (July 1987): 22.

To counter the pejorative use of the term "public relations," professionals need to live up to the standards of the PRSA Code.

70 Doyle, Andrea. "How Much Truth in PR? Reporter Cries 'Foul!'" *O'Dwyer's PR Services Report,* July 1988, 28.

According to PR leaders, releasing information selectively is acceptable because premature release sometimes causes harm, the press has no right to all information, and all information is slanted anyway.

71 Drew, Elizabeth. "Letter from Washington." *The New Yorker,* 26 May 1986, 92-96.

Charges of conflict of interest followed Michael Deaver after he left the Reagan White House to establish his own public relations firm, Michael K. Deaver & Associates. Deaver's critics complained that he traded on his close relationship with President Reagan and that he signed on clients indiscriminately. He dealt with the issue of acid rain on behalf of Canada, for example, despite his involvement in the issue during his White House years.

72 Durbin, William A. "Managing Issues Is Public Relations Responsibility." *pr reporter,* 15 May 1978, 4-5.

To manage issues more effectively, public relations should be proactive, anticipating issues where the corporation can make a difference; should avoid defensiveness; should realize that many public issues are pleas for quality; and should concentrate on ends rather than means.

73 "Elias Buchwald." *Jack O'Dwyer's Newsletter,* 21 December 1988, 8.

The PRSA Ethics Committee's investigation of a meeting with CIA Director William Casey to engineer public support for the Reagan administration's policies in Central America conflicts with the interests of the committee chairman, who works with two of the PR practitioners who attended the meeting.

74 "Ethical Concerns of U.S. Business Offer Openings for PR Leadership but 1/3 Say Issue 'Overblown.'" *PR Strategies USA,* 1-15 February 1988, n.p.

According to a survey of 1,082 corporate executives, business school deans, and members of Congress, overemphasis on short-term profits and disaffection with American institutions are the chief causes of unethical business practices. Most respondents believe that high ethical standards strengthen a business's competitiveness, that CEOs have the most influence on employees' standards, and that business people and business associations should subscribe to codes of ethics.

75 "Ethics and Public Relations Explored in Telecast." *Public Relations Journal* 19 (August 1963): 13-17.

This transcript of a telecast on KNBC, Los Angeles, entitled "Ethics and Public Relations," covers truth-telling and image making. The profession of law serves as an analogy for the practice of public relations.

76 "Ethics Are a Vital Concern to PR Execs." *PR News,* 10 July 1989, 2.

Most of the six hundred persons who responded to a survey at the 1989 International Association of Business Communicators convention believe that ethics affect a company's profits and reputation and that corporate executives are working to improve the ethical conduct in their companies.

77 "Ethics Codes a Growing Interest of Management, Corporations Seem More Committed Now than Ass'ns: Public Relations Ramifications Prime Motivator." *pr reporter,* 3 August 1981, 2-3.

The results of a questionnaire by Opinion Research Corporation suggest that individual corporations are more committed to and satisfied with written standards of conduct than associations are. Typically instigated to enhance public image, codes of ethics are designed as guidelines for professional responsibility.

78 "Ethics in US Public Relations: Trouble at the Top." *IPRA Review* 10 (November 1986): 9.

Anthony M. Franco, head of a large PR firm in Detroit, bought stock in a client company knowing that the company would be sold and that the stock would rise in value. Shortly afterward, he accepted the presidency of Public Relations Society of America, the Securities and Exchange Commission charged him with insider trading, and they signed a consent decree. Franco resigned as PRSA president, having fueled the criticism that public relations is rife with unethical behavior.

79 Evans, Laurence. *The Communication Gap: The Ethics and Machinery of Public Relations and Information.* London: Charles Knight & Co., 1973.

For the benefit of both business and the public, corporations need a communication policy that is integral to their operating procedures. Public relations should be headed by a senior-level employee who serves as an "information officer," not as a propagandist or a corporate lackey. The PR professional, bound by the Code of Conduct of the Institute of Public Relations, ensures that the public receives accurate, helpful information, because public relations, like business itself, serves the corporation by serving the customer.

80 Fairman, Milton. "A Saint for Madison Avenue." *Public Relations Journal* 17 (November 1961): 14-16.

In Italy, Saint Bernardine of Siena has been declared the patron saint of advertising and public relations. Bernardine, who lived in the fifteenth century, was a master showman who understood the power of language and symbols to move audiences. He acted from conscience and was enormously influential in his native Italy. Movements have been initiated in France, Belgium, and the Netherlands to have Bernardine named the patron saint of mass communicators in their nations.

81 Fenderson, Kendrick E. "Roots of Controversial Business Behavior." *Public Relations Journal* 34 (April 1978): 50-52.

Lessons from history are neither unambiguous nor absolute truth. Interpretations of the works of Charles Darwin, Sigmund Freud, Niccolò Machiavelli, Adam Smith, Thomas Hobbes, and G. Gordon Liddy illustrate the most basic PR mistake: miscommunication.

82 Finn, David. "Big Sell in the Cold War." *Saturday Review,* 10 October 1959, 13-15, 55.

The Soviets seem to be winning the PR battle between the East and the West because they have a good sense of dramatic timing, they seize the offensive, their government is in the "propaganda business" full-time, they have a clearly defined dream and the drive to reach it, and they have spent money in areas that have gained them attention. The solution to this requires that "dynamic and intuitive" leadership generate the headlines that will demonstrate the essential role of the free world.

83 Finn, David. "The Businessman and His Critics." *Saturday Review,* 12 September 1964, 60-65.

Business people need to be less concerned about profits and more concerned about the harm their products may cause. Rather than acting defensively, they need to listen to criticism and adopt practices that are in the public's welfare.

84 Finn, David. "Dilemmas in Corporate Communications." In The American Assembly, *The Ethics of Corporate Conduct*. Englewood Cliffs, N.J.: Prentice-Hall, 1977, 160-71.

Genuine ethical dilemmas face today's corporate communicator, and this scope extends beyond such questions as truth-in-advertising, full disclosure, and avoidance of conflict of interest. The image dilemma forces corporations to develop campaigns that reflect the true sentiments of the company, not those that the company thinks are desirable. The ego dilemma requires that corporate leaders become public figures, even though it may be more efficient for them to stay hidden in their offices. The dilemma of rational values forces the communicator to balance corporate views with personal convictions. Finally, the dilemmas of a critical press forces one to choose between the desire for favorable press and full disclosure of information.

85 Finn, David. "The Price of Corporate Vanity." *Harvard Business Review* 39 (July 1961): 135-43.

PR needs to reevaluate the soundness of image campaigns that rely solely on external appearances. Excessive concern with image leads to the beliefs that any problem is an image problem, that administrators should do what is popular rather than what is right, and that free public debate may be curtailed because companies do not release information that might hurt their image.

86 Finn, David. "Public Invisibility of Corporate Leaders." *Harvard Business Review* 58 (November/December 1980): 102-10.

Business leaders get bad press because they do not allow themselves to be seen as people. They need to be candid about their motives and let themselves be seen as human beings. They should integrate their business and personal lives, speak out for human values, initiate company programs that grow out of personal interests, develop their own style, and convince stockholders that managers have to be human beings first. If business leaders express the values they personally feel, the public will respond favorably.

87 Finn, David. "Stop Worrying about Your Image." *Harper's,* June 1962, 76-82.

As the image business has grown, so have ethical concerns and questions concerning its efficacy. Images have no impact without substance to back them, and there is little evidence that images can make or save a business. Image advertising may be popular because it hides inadequacies in organizations and their leaders and reflects the culture's search for meaning.

88 Finn, David. "Struggle for Ethics in Public Relations." *Harvard Business Review* 37 (January/February 1959): 49-58.

One of the major functions of a company's public relations activity is to help clarify the company's role in society. Clarification of issues such as artificial images, "prestige build-ups," campaign tactics and the purchase of publicity is essential if PR is to fulfill its social responsibility.

89 Finn, David. "The Struggle for Ethics." In *Information, Influence, & Communication: A Reader in Public Relations,* ed. Otto Lerginger and Albert J. Sullivan. New York: Basic Books, 1965, 467-79. Reprinted from David Finn, *Public Relations and Management* New York: Reinhold Publishing Corp., 1960, 145-65.

If top management can agree that it has a responsibility to the community, lower managers will be able to make ethical decisions that reflect this commitment.

The six areas of ethical conflict involve selling artificial images, building up products or programs to gain prestige, attempting to gain respect through influence, engineering public consent through PR techniques, telling the truth, and doing good for its own reward rather than for publicity. Top management should stimulate open discussion of these issues, and PR should encourage introspection and analysis.

90 Finn, David. "Why Business Has Trouble with the Media, and Vice Versa." *IPRA Review* 6 (Winter 1982): 22-27.

The relationship between representatives of the media and PR people is strained because legal restrictions sometimes prevent full disclosure, reporters are critical of business or do not understand it, and businesses are overly defensive, usually because they do not understand the press. More education on both sides is needed.

91 Fitzgerald, Stephen E. "Ethics." *Public Relations Journal* 7 (October 1951): 5-7, 12.

Ethics codes grant prestige to the practitioner, assurance to the client, and protection to the public. They represent a compromise between the need for public service and the need to make a living.

92 Forrestal, Dan J. "Written Word Basic Communications Key." *Editor & Publisher,* 6 November 1957, 18.

> Professional development needs to be strengthened in terms of the Code of Professional Standards and the mechanisms for its enforcement, PRSA publications, and membership standards.

93 Fox, James F. "Public Relations: Some Ethical Considerations." In *Ethics, Morality and the Media: Reflections on American Culture,* ed. Lee Thayer. New York: Hastings House, 1980, 153-62.

> Criticism of public relations is frequently self-contradictory because it comes from academics and journalists who work for organizations that engage in PR or because it calls for disclosure as it denounces a central channel of disclosure. Such criticism fails to recognize that public relations is a management function engaged more in advising than in promoting and that the Public Relations Society of America requires ethical conduct of its members. Justified criticism typically involves errant individuals or irresponsible businesses. Ultimately, society dictates standards for PR professionals to follow, and public relations practices will reflect the values of society.

94 Francis, John D. "A Look Beneath the Bottom Line." *Public Relations Journal* 46 (January 1990): 16-17, 32.

> A monomaniacal focus on short-term profit has made businesses socially irresponsible and has actually cost them money. Public relations counselors, with access both to the public and to the boardroom, can remedy the problem.

95 "Gelb's USIA Seriously Compromised." *Jack O'Dwyer's Newsletter,* 1 February 1989, 7.

> Bruce Gelb has been nominated to head the U.S. Information Agency (USIA), which is reeling from the disclosure that recently hired Walter Raymond is a former CIA agent. Both the USIA and Raymond have independently been associated with questionable activities.

96 Gildea, Robert L. "Doubting Thomas Our Patron Saint?" *Public Relations Quarterly* 22 (Spring 1977): 25-27.

> PR can help rebuild public confidence in organizations by standing up for principles and encouraging socially responsible action.

97 Gitter, A. George, and Engelina Jaspers. "Are PR Counselors Trusted Professionals?" *Public Relations Quarterly* 27 (Winter 1982): 28-30.

According to a survey of 227 undergraduates, college students learn to trust accountants and social workers and they learn to distrust salespersons and public relations practitioners.

98 Golden, L. L. L. *Only by Public Consent: American Corporations Search for Favorable Opinion.* New York: Hawthorn Books, 1968.
    Because businesses exist at the pleasure of the public, public acceptance and approval are essential to their profitable operation. Corporations such as AT&T, Du Pont, General Motors, Standard Oil Company (New Jersey), and U.S. Steel have learned that the basis of the public's acceptance of an institution is its performance. Public relations is thus a way of life, not a group of techniques. Corporate public relations interprets the company to the public and interprets public opinion to management. In this way, public interest can remain a daily concern of management.

99 Golden, L. L. L. "When Washington Investigates." *Saturday Review,* 8 December 1962, 70.
    Two investigations, one of PR's role in disseminating stock market information to the public, and the other of activities of PR firms in foreign governments, raise doubts regarding how ethical PR is.

100 Goodman, Ronald. "Back to Basics: Let's Tell the Truth." *Management World,* September 1979, 1, 18.
    For business to counter the lack of public credibility, they should report their activities clearly and honestly, admitting mistakes when they occur. Businesses should pay close attention to their publics' attitudes and produce products that they are willing to back fully.

101 Gordon, Gloria, and Cliff McGoon. "What Are the Issues that Will Shape 1987?" *Communication World,* January 1987, 12-19.
    In addition to professional credibility, mergers and takeovers, corporate down-sizing, consulting, international communication, technology, minority representation, communication overload, and crisis communication, codes of ethics are a major concern in public relations. Leaders in public relations are calling for the Public Relations Society of America and the International Association of Business Communicators to combine their codes of ethics and to sharpen their mechanisms for enforcement.

102 Goss, Bert C. "The Common Sense of PRSA's Financial Code." *Public Relations Journal* 20 (April 1964): 6-8.

The growth of financial PR prompted PRSA to work closely with the Securities and Exchange Commission to develop a Code of Financial Conduct. The code specifies that PRSA members are responsible for abiding by the rules of the SEC in letter and spirit, disclosing all information except when it is confidential, not violating confidentiality of privileged information, especially for personal gain, ensuring accuracy of released information, identifying sources of information, and rejecting compensation if positions would conflict with duties to the client, employer, or investing public.

103 Greggains, Brian C. "Beware the Hidden Persuaders." *Macleans,* 1 September 1980, 6.

Because the media have great social influence, they should select what publicity seekers they will accommodate carefully. Similarly, public relations professionals should exercise more imagination, seeking to motivate the public rather than simply copying techniques that have worked for others.

104 Grisdela, Cynthia S. "SEC Files Charges of Insider Trading against Publicist." *Wall Street Journal*, 27 August 1986, 4.

PRSA president Anthony Franco signed a consent decree with the Securities and Exchange Commission after charges that he used confidential information about the impending sale of his client, Cowley, Milner & Co. Franco purchased three thousand shares of Cowley stock, which rose from $41 to $48.25 a share.

105 Gross, Sidney. "Bill Moyers Tracks 'The Image Makers,'" *Public Relations Journal* 40 (June 1984): 19-20.

Bill Moyers's television show takes a responsible look at PR. The program highlights the work of Edward Bernays and Ivy Lee and reflects Moyers's concern with ethical problems.

106 Hamilton, Seymour. "PR Ethics, from Publicity to Interaction." *Public Relations Quarterly* 31 (Spring 1986): 15-19.

Grunig's types of public relations correlate with Sullivan's definitions of values in PR. Press agentry and public information models are guided by technical values. Something is good because it is competent or because it follows the rules for how something should be done. The two-way asymmetric model, the engineering of consent, is based on the value of loyalty to one's organization. In an extreme form, this perspective can lead to blind solidarity and groupthink. The two-way symmetric model, which works to create consensus between an organization and its publics, is guided by the promise of mutual values.

107 Harlow, Rex F. "A Plain Lesson We Should Heed." *Public Relations Journal* 5 (March 1949): 7-10.

Until a code of ethics or professional practices is adopted, PR practitioners should follow ten commonsense rules, including seeking truth and upholding PR's good name.

108 Harlow, Rex F. "Is Public Relations a Profession?" *Public Relations Quarterly* 14 (Winter 1970): 37.

Measured by seven criteria, public relations is an emerging profession. PR practitioners (1) are heterogeneous in their knowledge and community orientation, (2) share inadequacies that marked other emerging professions, (3) have a code of ethics that is too vague to apply to concrete cases, (4) have a professional association for purposes of identity and power, (5) identify standards of professional behavior with the caveat of a grandfather clause, (6) tie credentials to university education, and (7) try to persuade the public of the field's professionalism.

109 Harrington, Alan. *Life in the Crystal Palace.* New York: Alfred A. Knopf, 1959.

Harrington left corporate life after working for 3 1/2 years in the public relations department at the headquarters. Chapter 13, "Public Relations," argues that PR professionals do not lie; rather, they arrange true statements to gain public approval. As advocacy for hire, PR descends from the sophists. It can never be a profession like law or medicine because its foundation is fluid. Law serves justice and medicine humanity, but PR tampers with truth for the benefit of a client's image.

110 Harrison, Stanley L. "Ethics and Moral Issues in Public Relations Curricula." *Journalism Educator* 45 (Autumn 1990): 32-38.

A survey of 134 schools listed in the PRSA publication, *Where to Study Public Relations*, revealed that ethics is a major component in the study of public relations. However, PR textbooks typically treat ethics superficially: their ethics chapters are short, moralistic, and euphemistic. The study of public relations should include a rigorous course on ethics taught by well-trained and sensitive instructors.

111 Harrison, Stanley L. "Pedagogical Ethics for Public Relations and Advertising." *Journal of Mass Media Ethics* 5, no. 4 (1990): 256-62.

According to a survey of 134 college advertising and public relations programs, courses on ethics are required by 12 percent of schools, and they are usually taught under the auspices of journalism.

Although ethics is ostensibly taught across the communication curriculum, it is typically unsystematic and shallow.

112 Hathaway, James W. "Social Responsibility–Earning Credibility and Appreciation," *IPRA Review* 9 (February 1985): 18-20, 23.

Although socially responsible activities by business have increased markedly, the public remains largely unimpressed. The public seems to want corporations to promote health, the environment, honesty, fair employment, and resource conservation. Businesses must also let the public know about the socially responsible activities in which they are engaged.

113 Heath, Robert L. "Are Focus Groups a Viable Tool for PR Practitioners to Help Their Companies Establish Corporate Responsibility?" *Public Relations Quarterly* 32 (Winter 1987-88): 24-28.

The major task of the coming decade will be to develop methods for monitoring the standards of ethics held by the public. To develop ethical standards, companies must consider the fit between their interpretation of "ethical" and the ethical definitions held by the public. This monitoring must include both key publics and the "voiceless masses" whose opinions become important during public policy battles.

One way to monitor the ethical sensibilities of publics, especially those who lack visibility and vocal leadership, is to conduct regular focus groups. Focus groups can be especially helpful in clarifying four dimensions of public policy issues: likelihood, impact, timing, and potential for resolution. They can also be used to ask publics what they think constitutes ethical or unethical corporate behavior. One limitation of focus groups is that the group must reflect the larger population one is interested in monitoring, and the group must be well conducted.

114 Heath, Robert L., and Richard Alan Nelson. "Social Responsibility and Corporate Planning." In *Issues Management: Corporate Public Policymaking in an Information Society*. Beverly Hills: Sage, 1986, 139-60.

Managing issues requires integrating corporate activities with the public interest. Organizations must see themselves as vehicles for accomplishing social goals and recognize that the public distinguishes between legal and ethical behavior. They must create and follow a code of corporate responsibility based on public standards. The interrelationship between standards of social responsibility and corporate planning is illustrated by how Nestlé Corporation handled the controversy surrounding its marketing of infant formula in third world countries. Nestlé responded to negative public opinion by changing corporate policy once the issue of social responsibility became paramount.

115 Heath, Robert L., and Michael Ryan. "Public Relations' Role in Defining Corporate Social Responsibility." *Journal of Mass Media Ethics* 4, no. 1 (1989): 21-38.

Corporations should monitor their environments to identify publics' values and establish ethical behaviors based on the results. Results from eighty-two corporations responding to a survey on their codes for conduct and their monitoring activities indicated that most of them do have codes of social responsibility and that most attempt to monitor community standards for corporate behavior. However, internal publics are monitored more often than external ones: most information about social responsibility issues is generated from techniques such as networking, internal focus groups, and internal panels of experts. A large minority of companies has no apparatus to monitor public standards.

116 Hickey, Brian. "A Ticket to Ride?" *Public Relations Journal* 43 (January 1987): 8-9.

PRSA's Code of Professional Standards prohibits members from providing trips for media representatives that are unrelated to legitimate news interest, yet many corporations continue to offer to pay for all or part of the expenses journalists accrue when attending an event. Walt Disney Company invited top entertainers, celebrities, public officials, and countless reporters to celebrate its fifteenth anniversary. The weekend event included press conferences and interviews with celebrities and Disney officials, as well as a press handbook that included story ideas and a list of prepared print and broadcast pieces and photographs. Disney's philosophy is that "you have to see Disney, that you have to experience it," and the company chairman has said that Disney will continue to offer invited guests the option of paying or not paying part or all of their costs.

117 Hiebert, Ray E. "Public Relations Ethics." *Social Science Monitor* 11 (August 1989): 1-3.

A recent issue of *Public Relations Review* devoted to ethical behavior reported that PR people have strong religious values but a situational socioeconomic morality, that PR people who are concerned about social responsibility more frequently participate in organizational policy meetings, that some college PR people admit to some unethical practices, and that surveys of business people and students indicate that PR people are seen as "fairly ethical."

118 Hill, Don. "Standing in Loco Clientis." *Public Relations Journal* 41 (June 1985): 4-5.

The rules for ethical behavior are not clear-cut, and even a comprehensive code of ethics cannot cover all situations. No law or code of ethics requires PR people to behave "in loco clientis" the way doctors and lawyers must, but PR people can choose to practice that way.

119 Hill, John W. "The Future of Public Relations." *Public Relations Journal* 21 (September 1965): 10-13.

Public relations has made great strides toward achieving the status of a profession, but PR is still criticized for unethical practices and still needs to deal with the fact that anyone can claim to be a PR expert. Correcting these difficulties requires a code of ethics and an accreditation plan for undergraduate and postgraduate programs at universities.

120 Hodges, Louis W., Alan D. Galletly, Jeffrey G. Hanna, Frank French, and Hugh M. Culbertson. "A Blown Safe at the Phone Company." *Journal of Mass Media Ethics* 5, no. 4 (1990): 263-69.

In response to a hypothetical case in which a PR director leaked a story to the press in defiance of her supervisor's order, three respondents argued that she jeopardized her integrity and one argued that she served the best long-term interests of her company, employees, and customers.

121 Holmes, Paul. "Public Relations." *Adweek's Marketing Week,* 11 September 1989, 234-35.

Demand for ethical accountability and a growing sophistication in getting publicity will combine to allow PR to take the lead in monitoring issues and formulating corporate policy in the coming decade. Changes in corporate environments will require that they receive more strategic advice on issues than ever before.

122 Horton, Thomas R. "Villainy & Heroism in the Executive Suite." *Management Review* 76 (September 1987): 5.

Businesses need to be more candid with the press to brighten their tarnished image.

123 "HUD Audit Puts Spotlight on L.I. Press/PR Setup." *O'Dwyer's PR Services Report,* September 1989, 16-19.

The question of dual ownership of newspapers and PR firms was highlighted recently when HUD disallowed $38,864 paid by the village of Hempstead, New York, to the *Long Island Business News* whose editor is also chairman of a local PR firm. HUD apparently opposed paying two firms for PR at the same time. According to Paul Townsend, chairman of Townsend Communications and editor of *Long Island Business News*, the payments to the paper were made for PR advice, not coverage of stories in *LIBN*. Townsend denies the claim of several ex-staffers that his PR clients receive more mentions in the paper. He notes that the circulation of the paper would not be climbing if the paper was not credible.

124 Hunt, Todd. "Will Ethical Behavior Benefit an Organization? Students Can Learn by Trying to Convince Others." *Public Relations Research & Education* 1 (1984): 56-59.

Because ethical standards emerge by involvement in a society that shares values and norms, students can begin to learn how to handle ethical problems in an organization by participating in complex public relations problems. In a memo to an executive, students are to object to an organization's practice without lecturing, assuming shared beliefs, or exercising faulty logic. Their memos must relate ethical behavior to the long-term goals of the organization, illustrate possible outcomes, and explain the costs and benefits of ethical choices.

125 Huntsinger, Jerry. "More on Ethics and Fundraising Letters." *NonProfit Times,* October 1989, 42.

Respondents to a poll on ethics and fund-raising letters complained about such practices as telemarketing, compensation for executives, shared mailing lists between charity and commercial organizations, corporate name changes following bad publicity, the use of "official carrier envelopes" for routine fund-raising, and phony matching-fund campaigns.

126 Huntsinger, Jerry. "Readers Cast Their Votes on Ethical Issues." *NonProfit Times,* September 1989, 32.

Most of the nearly five hundred readers of *NonProfit Times* who responded to a straw poll on ethical issues related to fund-raising letters opposed the transfer of donor names without the donors' permission and the use of phrases such as "I am writing you this personal letter" in mass mailings. Readers also said that donors should be advised regarding the portion of their gift that is not tax-deductible when a premium is offered in return for a gift. These responses run counter to common practices.

127 "Imagemakers Fight Their Own Bad Image." *Industry Week,* 22 June 1970, 40-43.

Public relations will be only as good as top management allows it to be. Top management must allow the PR staff to serve as advisers, not just communicators, demand evaluation of PR programs, including those that fail, and cooperate with PR people to develop a corporate image.

128 "In Conference & Survey, CPRS Asks: Are We Developing Strategic, Ethical Practitioners to Meet New Demand for Senior Positions?" *pr reporter,* 26 June 1989, 1-2.

At the Conference of the Canadian Public Relations Society, practitioners discussed results of a survey that indicated that most practitioners do not think most of their peers hold professional values, follow ethics codes, or integrate scholarly work into a conceptual framework. Further, survey respondents believed that though public education is growing, little theory and research is taught. Proposed solutions include better training programs, increased professional status, and an approach to problem solving that does not require cover-up tactics.

129 "IRS Closes Amidei Firm in S.F." *Jack O'Dwyer's Newsletter,* 20 September 1989, 7.

The IRS closed Amidei & Co., a San Francisco firm headed by L. Neal Amidei, for nonpayment of back taxes. Although Amidei said that he was negotiating with the IRS, the IRS said that it told Amidei a year ago that it would seize the property if taxes were not paid. The total debt owed to the IRS could be nearly $200,000, and according to insiders the firm also owed money to suppliers. According to John Paluszek, president of PRSA, these allegations "require review under our ethics code."

130 Jensen, Donald L. "Just What Is a PR Man, Anyway?" *Advanced Management* 24 (May 1959): 12-13.

If public relations is to be recognized as a profession, its national organizations must guarantee that PR comes to mean "truth, well told."

131 Joffe, Bruce H. "Law, Ethics and Public Relations." *Public Relations Journal* 45 (July 1989): 38-40.

PR writers must be aware of the laws and ethics that govern written works. They should be aware of new copyright laws that give rights to the creator of a work unless such rights are waived. If requested to make extensive revisions, writers should ask for a guarantee that their work will be used. Also, they should be careful to avoid conflicts of interest in cases where they are working for more than one party, especially when dual payments may be involved.

132 Jordan, Myron K. "FDR's Condemnation of Electric Utility Public Relations." *Public Relations Review* 15 (Summer 1989): 41-51.

In FDR's 1932 presidential campaign, he condemned the electric utilities public relations campaign for deluging the media with press releases, creating nationwide committees to carry out the campaign, hiring newspaper people to conduct programs aimed at newspapers, entertaining newspeople by buying them dinner, theater tickets, and drinks, sponsoring editorial clip sheets without disclosing that sponsorship, and buying enormous amounts of ad space that intimidated newspapers into using utility news. Close examination of the campaign, however, indicates that the utility companies did nothing illegal, that at least half the charges were based on inaccuracies, and that although some aspects of the campaign would be considered unethical by 1980s' standards, they were common practice in the 1920s. Furthermore, whereas PR may have been "hypocritical" by using information without disclosing sponsorship or source, the newspapers showed themselves to be "corruptible."

133 Judd, Larry R. "Credibility, Public Relations and Social Responsibility." *Public Relations Review* 15 (Summer 1989): 34-39.

A survey of one hundred PR practitioners found a significant relationship between recommending socially responsible actions and participating in policy decisions. Respondents also indicated that responsibility to society was more important than responsibility to the employer or client. Few respondents thought they would be perceived as more credible than a chief executive or journalist. When asked to compare the moral standards of PR with those of twenty-five other professions, respondents ranked PR in the lower half. Most frequently, honesty was named as the quality that would improve credibility.

134 "Judicial Council." *Editor & Publisher,* 5 March 1960, 34.

The newly revised Code of Professional Standards for the Practice of Public Relations will be enforced by forty-eight PRSA members who were named to the National Judicial Council. The council is divided into eight panels, one for each PRSA district. The council will consider complaints and code violations and can recommend penalties to the PRSA Board of Directors.

135 Jurgensen, John H., and James Lukaszewski. "Ethics: Content before Conduct." *Public Relations Journal* 44 (March 1988): 47-48.

Ethical thought must go beyond codes of ethics to find the principles that serve as the foundation for moral decision making. These foundational purposes and principles are not situational, but are embedded in time-honored cultural norms.

136 Katz, David M. "Spin Control: No Substitute for Risk Control." *National Underwriter,* 4 April 1988, 9-11.

Unlike Johnson & Johnson, which earned high praise and increased its market share by recalling Tylenol and replacing capsules with caplets after users of Tylenol died from poisoning, Ashland Oil responded to its oil spill in the Monongehela River with publicity strategies and contingency plans only, rejecting strong preventive measures as "not practicable."

137 Klein, Joan Dempsey. "Personal Dilemma: Situational Ethics and Flexible Morality in America." *Public Relations Journal* 32 (August 1976): 10-13.

A generalized set of ethical standards must be flexible enough to change with time and situations. Honesty and integrity should be close to the top of any list of ethical absolutes.

138 Kleiner, Art. "The Public Relations Coup." *Adweek's Marketing Week,* 16 January 1989, 20-23.

Whether by video news releases or through corporate-sponsored talk-show appearances, public relations firms often promote products under the guise of information programming.

139 Knott, Leonard L. *Plain Talk about Public Relations.* Toronto: McClelland and Stewart, 1961.

Although the essence of good public relations is sincerity, too many practitioners promulgate false or misleading information and obtain coverage by bribery. These widespread practices threaten the reputation of business, conditioning the public to disbelieve whatever business has to say. Ultimately, the misbehavior of business jeopardizes the very system of free enterprise. Businesses need a good reputation to survive, and that requires that they change their philosophy. Businesses need to adopt policies that serve employees, shareholders, suppliers, consumers, and the public at large, provide quality goods and services at fair prices, and publicize these policies and products. By making known their good intentions and good deeds, businesses create in the public mind a good reputation for themselves as well as for business as a whole. Adopting high standards of morality requires that businesses voluntarily accept an enforceable code of ethics similar to those that the professions support.

140 Koten, John A. "Moving toward Higher Standards for American Business." *Public Relations Review* 12 (Fall 1986): 3-11.

Today's corporate communicator can help restore business to a prominent role in society by remembering that corporate performance is an expression of character and the corporation must operate in the public interest.

Arthur W. Page, America's first vice president of PR at AT&T, articulated six standards that are as applicable today as they were during the 1920s: (1) be attentive to the public; (2) be honest; (3) ensure that the company "does," not just "tells;" (4) manage for tomorrow; (5) help the company realize that the public controls the corporate fate; and (6) interject the best personal character into corporate character. To achieve these standards, corporate communicators need to be involved in top level decision making and educate future communicators not just in the techniques but in economics, politics, literature, and history.

141 Kruckeberg, Dean. "The Need for an International Code of Ethics." *Public Relations Review* 15 (Summer 1989): 6-17.

Public relations practitioners of transnational corporations should subscribe to an international code of ethics because transnational corporations have been accused of graft and corruption and of violating public interest in the areas of environment and human safety, politics and humanitarian issues, and consumer affairs. An international code would help to resolve the inherent moral dilemmas of worldwide relationships. Although there is no objective way to determine the relative merit of different moral systems, an international code for professional communicators would provide guidelines for practitioners, illustrate what clients and supervisors should expect from practitioners, provide a basis for charges that wrongdoing has occurred, and provide a defense against charges of wrongdoing.

142 Kruckeberg, Dean, and Kenneth Starck. *Public Relations and Community: A Reconstructed Theory.* New York: Praeger, 1988.

Public relations emerged because of consumerism and the loss of community resulting from new means of communication and transportation. However, public relations early adopted principles rooted in persuasion and advocacy rather than principles based on social involvement and participation. PR remains a vocation utilizing persuasion to obtain a vested goal on behalf of a client. The Chicago School of Social Thought offers a remedy, largely on the basis of sense of community. The Chicago School would encourage public relations to understand communication as doing something communicatively with someone rather than to someone, so that public relations could be practiced with an overall goal of restoring and maintaining community. The public relations practitioner becomes a communication facilitator who can help build a sense of community among organizations and their geographic publics by helping community members and the organizations they represent become conscious of common interests that underlie both their contentions and their solutions, encouraging leisure-time activities of citizens, leading their organizations in charitable works, and helping the community share aesthetic experiences. The Amoco refinery at Sugar Creek, Missouri (1904-82), serves as a case study.

143 Lee, Burns W. "Code Enforcement Machinery Adopted." *Public Relations Journal* 7 (20 December 1951): 28-29.
The several hundred PRSA members who attended the annual business meeting unanimously approved changes in the by-laws to specify the procedure by which those who violate professional standards are judged and punished.

144 Lewis, Diane E. "PR's Founder also Its Conscience." *Boston Globe,* 4 October 1990, 33, 36.
Ninety-eight-year-old Edward L. Bernays, who has long championed the use of celebrities, experts, and social science in public relations, advocates licensing, registration, and academic preparation for admission into the practice of public relations.

145 Lipman, Joanne. "PR Society Receives Some Very Bad PR – From Its Ex-Chief." *Wall Street Journal,* 26 September 1986, 1, 22.
Former PRSA president Anthony Franco accepted his position while an SEC investigation for insider trading was pending. He failed to inform the PRSA, so that when news of the investigation broke, most PRSA members found out through news reports. And when Franco resigned, the PRSA failed to send press releases.

146 Logsdon, Jeanne M., and David R. Palmer. "Issues Management and Ethics." *Journal of Business Ethics* 7 (March 1988): 191-98.

Issues management is gaining in popularity as a way for corporations to monitor the environment and to fulfill their social obligations. This latter function assumes that firms are basing decisions on ethical norms and not simply using issues management as a tool to promote the firm's economic self-interest. By combining a comprehensive corporate ethic, stakeholder analysis, and social vision, organizations can use issues management in responsible ways.

147 Manne, Henry G. "The Myth of Corporate Responsibility." *Public Relations Journal* 26 (December 1970): 6-8.

The best way to achieve corporate responsibility is to rely upon market forces.

148 Markley, Herbert E. "A CEO Looks at Public Relations in the '80s." *Public Relations Journal* 35 (September 1979): 11-14.

In the coming decade, CEOs can expect greater professionalism from their public relations people. This increased professionalism requires the exercise of good judgment, advance planning, and access to top executives.

149 Marston, John. "There's Nothing Wrong with Persuasion." *Public Relations Quarterly* 4 (January 1959): 17-21.

To merit public acceptance of persuasion, persons working in the persuasive arts should use good taste in their messages, establish standards, and cease infighting among various persuasive media. To gain that acceptance they must devise more ways of rewarding uses of persuasion that serve the public good, do more public service as individuals, and be people of character and courage.

150 Matrat, Lucien. "Ethics and Doubts." *IPRA Review* 10 (November 1986): 17-20.

Trust, the ultimate goal of PR, can be achieved only if the profession is regulated by a code of ethics that protects the sacred character of the human person by regulating the behavior that one human being should adopt toward another. The Code of Athens is such an ethical code. It is linked to the U.N. Declaration of Human Rights and has been translated into twenty-two languages.

151 McAfee, J. Wesley. "Public Relations – Techniques or Ethics?" *Public Relations Journal* 10 (February 1954): 7-8, 29..

Democracy is dependent on publicity. Although no code of ethics is perfect, PRSA provides leadership and performs a public service so that the dangers of publicity can be controlled.

152 McBride, Genevieve. "Ethical Thought in Public Relations History: Seeking a Relevant Perspective." *Journal of Mass Media Ethics* 4, no. 1 (1989): 5-20.

Ivy Lee and Edward Bernays left distinctly different ethical legacies. Lee supported the journalistic ideal of "objectivity," whereas Bernays promoted principles of advocacy. Called to emulate both Lee and Bernays, practitioners are "caught in an ethical quandary." Since PR has different goals than journalism, objectivity is impossible for PR practitioners to achieve. Most PR people have been trained in journalistic traditions, but journalists cannot fully legitimize PR without admitting that their ethic is not universal but native only to the nature of their work. This leads both PR people and journalists to think less of the PR field.

Bernays' alternative conception of the PR person as advocate defined "ethical" by the results that PR work would accomplish. Bernays countered the prevailing journalistic perspective on PR, seeing PR as a profession with the legitimate purpose of advocacy and an ethical perspective of its own.

153 McCammond, Donald B. "A Matter of Ethics." *Public Relations Journal* 39 (November 1983): 46-47.

The Code of Professional Standards for the Practice of Public Relations was adopted in 1959 by the PRSA Board of Directors and ratified by the assembly in 1960. The Grievance Board was established in 1962. The board acts as an investigative body, similar to a grand jury. The board acts on complaints or may instigate investigations on its own, it reviews evidence on the validity of alleged violations, and determines how the code should be applied to the charge.

The Grievance Board may refer a complaint to a district judicial panel for hearing and judgment, it may dismiss the complaint, it may suspend the complaint pending the outcome of a civil or criminal court proceeding, or it may withdraw the complaint following an amicable settlement.

Questions raised before the board in the last year have included such things as whether a practitioner can guarantee a certain number of media placements, how the APR and member PRSA designations can be used, and who legally owns the records in a practitioner-employer-client relationship.

154 McCammond, Donald B. "The Right Choice." *Public Relations Journal* 43 (February 1987): 8-10.

According to the PRSA Code of Professional Standards, PR practitioners (1) should realize that confidentiality of client information may sometimes conflict with the requirement to divorce oneself from clients involved in illegal activities, (2) may not use confidential information to the disadvantage of potential clients, (3) cannot serve an undisclosed special interest, (4) cannot set up an organization that purports to serve an independent cause but actually carries out a private or unannounced interest of a PRSA member, client, or employer, (5) must sever relationships with a client who is presenting false and misleading information, (6) can keep appreciative payments from colleagues, as long as the client is aware, (7) cannot disclose financial or takeover information about clients to friends or colleagues, and (8) cannot knowingly present false or misleading information to the public.

155 McCammond, Donald B. "Take-Home Quiz." *Public Relations Journal* 43 (January 1987): 7.

The ethical choice is not always immediately clear in many PR situations. Readers are encouraged to think about how they would handle eight situations involving privileged information and conflicts of interest.

156 McCann, Thomas P. *An American Company: The Tragedy of United Fruit.* New York: Crown, 1976.

In this insider's history of the United Fruit Company, the former director of public relations and company vice president denounces many of the company's public relations strategies. During the McCarthy era, for instance, when United Fruit produced a film entitled *Why the Kremlin Hates Bananas*, Edward L. Bernays directed the company's attempt to convince U.S. citizens that the interests of the banana and sugar company were identical to the interests of the United States. The overthrow of the pro-land reform government of Guatemala was due largely to a partnership between United Fruit and the CIA. Favorable press coverage followed press junkets to Guatemala, when, for instance, *New York Times* publisher Arthur Sulzberger witnessed a "communist riot." Soviet weapons were placed in the hands of slain government soldiers, and their "discovery" was promptly announced to the press. A few weeks after the overthrow, when the Justice Department initiated an antitrust suit against United Fruit, Bernays convinced many newspapers that communist infiltration in the government was responsible for the action against the CIA's ally.

After an earthquake in Managua killed thousands and left more homeless, the company, then called United Brands, sponsored the Nicaraguan Earthquake Emergency Drive, which raised $25,000 for disaster relief. United Brands contributed about $5,000 to the drive, but it spent $50,000 in advertising and promotion. These and other examples of dishonesty and impropriety led McCann to conclude, "The more I thought about it, and the more I looked at the events around me, the more certain I became that public relations was helping to screw up the world. In back of almost every bad situation, every lie, every injustice, I could see the hand of the PR man pulling the strings, making things happen, covering things up. Public relations had taken over the government, the prisons, the protest movement, even the ecology" (p. 152).

157 McIntyre, Robert B. "Honest PR Helps Clients and Media." *Editor & Publisher*, 6 April 1963, 54-55.

Newspaper-reporter-turned-PR-practitioner Joseph F. Quinn criticizes PR people who exaggerate their capabilities in order to land an account or who fail to distinguish between news and puffery. On the positive side, honest PR serves clients and the media by providing news of products and corporation activities, which the public wants and needs to know about.

158 McIntyre, Robert B. "PR Man's Conscience Called His Only Guide." *Editor & Publisher*, 10 June 1961, 36.

In order to perform services for both corporate management and the press, public relations must be sure that the corporation has a product or idea worth promoting and that it deals with the press honestly.

159 McKee, Blaine K., Oguz B. Nayman, and Dan L. Lattimore. "How PR People See Themselves." *Public Relations Journal* 31 (November 1975): 47-52.

Survey results indicate that most public relations practitioners see themselves as professionals. Since these people are more likely to act like professionals, this can be taken as an indication that PR is moving closer toward professional status.

160 McKee, James E., Jr. "The PRSA Grievance Board." *Public Relations Journal* 27 (June 1971): 18-21.

The enforcement mechanism of the Code of Professional Standards of the Public Relations Society of America is stronger than that of several other professional associations including the American

Society of Newspaper Editors, the Motion Picture Association of America, the Comics Magazine Association of America, the National Association of Broadcasters, and the American Association of Advertising Agencies. The power of the PRSA to enforce professionalism is similar to that of the American Bar Association. The Grievance Board of the PRSA has examined thirty-six cases involving questionable practices of PRSA members in nine years. The Grievance Board investigates and prosecutes cases of code violation. PRSA by-laws require that no publicity be given to actions of the Grievance Board, and its members are bound to confidentiality. Although this secrecy is necessary to protect the rights and reputations of members, PRSA members often do not know much about the board's activities.

161 Mechling, Thomas B. "The Mythical Ethics of Law, PR and Accounting." *Business and Society Review,* Winter 1976-77, 6-10.

Lawyers, accountants, and PR people have elaborate codes of ethics, but they serve mainly as a screen from public review. The codes look good on paper, but they are seldom enforced. Article 15 of the PRSA vode, for example, requires a member to sever relationships with any client or employer if continuing the relationship would involve violating any principles of the code. This article is rarely invoked, despite the eighty corporations that have been convicted of illegal contributions, bribes, and kickbacks. Similarly, over one hundred lawyers were involved in Watergate and only six of them were disbarred, and the American Institute of Certified Public Accountants found Nixon's secretary of commerce and reelection finance chairman, who pleaded guilty to five counts of receiving illegal campaign contributions, not guilty of unethical conduct.

162 Mechling, Thomas B. "PR for Professionals." *Public Relations Journal* 26 (August 1970): 10-11.

Because the ethical codes of such professional organizations as the American Bar Association and the American Institute of Certified Public Accountants prohibit advertising or publicizing services, professional PR counseling is required to inform publics about the activities of associated firms. New avenues to carry these organizations' messages include professional speech making and article writing by members of the organization and expanded use of corporate newsletters and trade publications to cover these speeches and articles. Firms that communicate ethically with outside publics become recognized as important information sources.

163 Medlock, Julie. "Our Challenging Future." *Public Relations Journal* 4 (November 1948): 30-32.

The public relations profession faces its greatest challenge in using its special knowledge, tools, and techniques to support positions and leaders who are working to better the lot of humankind. By teaching clients and the public to think in terms of the public interest, PR fulfills its ethical responsibility and reaches its potential as a profession.

164 Modoux, Alain. "Is There a Place for Public Relations in Democratic Communications." *IPRA Review* 8 (February 1984): 9-11.

Public relations is a democratic profession because it recognizes the freedoms of thought, expression, and association as fundamental human rights and because it engages in true dialogue between publics.

165 Montgomery, Jim. "The Image Makers: In Public Relations, Ethical Conflicts Pose Continuing Problems." *Wall Street Journal,* 1 August 1978, 1, 14.

Ethical problems vex middle management PR practitioners who are pressured to produce. They are often told to withhold news until a more fortuitous time, to tell less than they know, or to refuse to give details of events. One annual report buried so much information that a Wall Street analyst accused it of being fraudulent.

Some PR people follow orders, some blow the whistle, and others give up their jobs in protest. PR people pay a price with the sixth highest admission rates to mental health institutions.

166 Moskowitz, Milton. "Trumpeting the New Values." *Communication World,* November 1983, 39-41.

To serve business well, mission statements have to be well articulated, credible, and based on what the corporate beliefs really are.

167 Moss, Edward K. "Is Public Relations a Profession?" *Public Relations Journal* 6 (October 1950): 7-8, 10.

Although many PR people are professional and honest, too many PR practitioners do not tell the truth and do not work for socially desirable ends. If PR is to grow as a profession, more thought must be given to ethical standards, and professional conduct must be achieved in daily practice.

168 Mullin, Stanley H. "Boundaries for Public Relations." *Public Relations Journal* 16 (November 1960): 18, 20.

Because PR's function is to guide management in solving and preventing relational problems, the boundaries of PR should be justice and good communication based on good character.

169 Nayman, Oguz, Blaine K. McKee, and Dan L. Lattimore. "PR Personnel and Print Journalists: A Comparison of Professionalism." *Journalism Quarterly* 54 (Autumn 1985): 492-97.

Two surveys comparing Colorado news and PR people found the PR practitioners to be slightly more educated, older, and better paid than newspersons. Nearly two-thirds of the PR people had previously worked in media and 55 percent of newspersons said they would consider moving into PR. Although both groups value professional attributes of their jobs, PR people indicated more job satisfaction.

170 Nelkin, Dorothy. "Managing Biomedical News." *Social Research* 55 (Autumn 1985): 625-46.

Because journalists shape public consciousness and set the agenda for policy on medical and scientific research, physicians and scientists try to manage the news by packaging information to convey the most positive image. They employ PR activities to encourage public support, influence public policy, enhance institutional prestige, and establish a competitive advantage. For the public to deepen its understanding of modern medicine, medical institutions need to allow journalists more open access to information, and they must restrict promotional activities. Journalists must critically examine information and work to convey understanding as well as information in the stories they write.

171 "Newspaper Publicizes PRSA 'Ethics Tussle,'" *O'Dwyer's PR Services Report,* July 1989, 43.

The *Legal Times*, a weekly circulation of eleven thousand, covered a decision by the PRSA Ethics Board to dismiss charges against four PRSA members, who were accused of giving PR advice to CIA head William Casey, and to investigate Summer Harrison who filed the complaint for breaching confidentiality rules.

172 "No Code Violation in CIA Meeting, Says PRSA." *O'Dwyer's PR Services Report,* May 1989, 18, 61.

The Board of Ethics and Professional Standards of PRSA unanimously agreed that four members who met with CIA head William Casey did not violate the ethics code.

173 Nolan, Joseph. "Business Beware: Early Warning Signs in the Eighties." *Public Opinion* 4 (April/May 1981): 14-17, 57.

To anticipate the public interest, businesses must identify social trends quickly, monitor social and political developments and integrate them into the management planning system, and act quickly on emerging issues.

A survey of over two thousand individuals indicated that gaps between what people thought they were entitled to have and what they did have were widest in the areas of people, work issues, safety, and well-being.

174 Northington, Suzanne. "'Our Chairman Says . . .': When Corporate PR People Make Up Quotes." *Christian Science Monitor,* 3 May 1988, 12.

PR people often invent quotes and attribute them to the CEO or other high-ranking official because the official is unavailable for comment or because the words need to be remarkable. PR people tend to see a quotation as a statement of the corporate viewpoint but emphasize that quotations should be approved by the person to whom they are attributed before being released to the press. Because Larry Speaks did not get President Reagan's approval before releasing quotes, his action was problematic.

175 "NSC Tapped PR Expertise a Second Time." *Jack O'Dwyer's Newsletter,* 9 November 1988, 7-8.

Four PRSA members were tapped by late CIA director William Casey for advice on a PR campaign to win support for U.S. policies in Central America. PR counselor Phil Lesly commented that this was a complex situation because Casey served in several administration positions simultaneously. It would have been improper to meet with Casey in his role as CIA head, but it was acceptable to talk to him in another role.

176 O'Dwyer, Jack, and Jerry Walker. "PR Played Major Role in Events of Iran-Contra Affair." *O'Dwyer's PR Services Report,* January 1989, 1, 32-45.

The involvement of five PR people who advised William Casey and the major role PR played in the Iran-contra affair raise serious ethical issues. When does an information and education campaign become illegal? What rights do PR people have to attempt to sway the American public on a complicated foreign policy issue?

177 Olasky, Marvin N. "The Aborted Debate within Public Relations: An Approach through Kuhn's Paradigm." In *Public Relations Research*

Annual 1, ed. James E. Grunig and Larissa A. Grunig. Hillsdale, N.J.: Erlbaum Associates, 1989, 87-95.

Critical examination of the purpose of public relations was aborted twenty-five years ago by those who enjoyed the profits the burgeoning field was producing. This resistance to development of a new philosophical paradigm for PR – one that rejected subjective emphasis on adaptation and mass psychology and upheld the search for objective truth – escalated the loss of credibility for the field as a whole.

Because current PR has destructive practical applications, a new debate is needed.

178 Olasky, Marvin N. "Abortion Rights: Anatomy of a Negative Campaign." *Public Relations Review* 13 (Fall 1987): 12-23.

A negative publicity campaign waged by prochoice groups against the "deceptiveness" of a prolife counseling center raises three ethical issues. First, this campaign made it seem as though all prolife centers were deceptive rather than the 5 percent specifically at fault. Second, the negative publicity campaign was supported by several large nonprofit prochoice groups; their opponent was a relatively small nonprofit group. Finally, this instance of a nonprofit group generating a campaign specifically designed to reduce the effectiveness of organizations with a different philosophy suggests that using top-notch public relations skills might stifle open debate on social issues.

179 Olasky, Marvin N. "Chemical Giant Hoodwinks the Press." *Business and Society Review,* Summer 1985, 60-63.

A chemical company with a history of employee cancer cooperated with the union to divert a newspaper reporter who was on to an explosive story. She finally filed an innocuous account that was buried on page 37.

180 Olasky, Marvin N. *Corporate Public Relations: A New Historical Perspective.* Hillsdale, N.J.: Lawrence Erlbaum Associates, 1987.

PR, which has undermined competition and threatened free enterprise, is now in the untenable position of balancing the corporation's need for privacy against the public's demand to know.

Resolving this ethical dilemma will involve reasserting "private relations" for business. To develop into a new discipline, PR requires (1) no government "tampering" with an individual industry, (2) minimal PR staff support for corporations, (3) courses for PR students that examine the impact of PR on society, and (4) honesty as an essential principle of communication.

181 Olasky, Marvin N. "Inside the Amoral World of Public Relations: Truth Molded for Corporate Gain." *Business and Society Review,* Winter 1985, 41-44.

According to interviews at a major corporation, PR people will not tell an outright lie but instead will focus attention on certain preferred issues. Practitioners feel uncomfortable with this process of diversion, but they feel that it is necessitated by managers and by an overeager but lax press.

182 Olasky, Marvin N. "Ministers or Panderers: Issues Raised by the Public Relations Society Code of Standards." *Journal of Mass Media Ethics* 1 (Fall/Winter 1985-86): 43-49.

PRSA's Code of Professional Standards is seldom enforced and is used as a shield rather than as a true code of ethics. The code must be strengthened first by defining "responsibility to the public" not as conforming to generally accepted standards or to public opinion polls but according to principles for determining right from wrong. In addition, the code can be strengthened by enforcing severe penalties for code violations, assigning public relations monitors, and assigning investigative business reporters to cover corporate events.

183 Olasky, Marvin N. "Public Relations vs. Private Enterprise: An Enlightening History which Raises Some Basic Questions." *Public Relations Quarterly* 30 (Winter 1985-86): 6-13.

From railroads in the late nineteenth century to steel companies in the late twentieth, public relations has sought government intervention in private enterprise. Success brought dire long-term results: less competition, industrial failure, and corporate dishonesty. Businesses should pare their PR staffs to a minimum and concentrate their efforts on producing and selling goods with little government involvement.

184 Olasky, Marvin N. "The 1984 Public Relations Scam Awards." *Business and Society Review,* Fall 1984, 42-46.

Recent corporate PR deceptions illustrate the duplicity of public relations. After Continental Airlines declared bankruptcy to break union contracts, it began proclaiming corporate democracy. Upjohn donated $4 million to the American Diabetes Association to increase opposition to the warnings the Food and Drug Administration mandated that its diabetes medications must carry. U.S. Steel won the federal quotas on imported steel that it sought after its negotiations to import finished steel from British Steel Corporation fell through; also, after announcing its policy of investing in steel, U.S. Steel paid a half billion dollars for Husky Oil's oil and gas acreage. Although banks convinced Congress to give the International Monetary Fund $8 billion to keep third-world nations from defaulting on their loans owed to U.S. banks, they continue to lend money to third-world countries. Finally, using the rhetoric of private enterprise, businesses have sought corporate welfare in both the National Industrial Policy and "public-private partnership."

185 Olasky, Marvin N. "The Public Relations Scams of 1985." *Business and Society Review,* Winter 1986, 52-55.
　　　　Several examples of corporate duplicity are illustrated in detail.

186 Olasky, Marvin N. "'Would I Lie?' Moral Pitfalls of Public Relations." *Eternity,* April 1986, 24-27.
　　　　Public relations is a utilitarian enterprise dominated by an "ideology of lying." It falls far short of the biblical ideal of being truthful both in intent and in behavior because it deifies the voice of the people. Although most PR practitioners fall sway to the ideology of lying, a few do not. The virtuous are those who obey godly principles and do not cater to the whims of public opinion.

187 Paget-Cooke, R. A. "Public Relations . . . A Bulwark of Democracy." *Public Relations Quarterly* 4 (Fall 1960): 11-15.
　　　　Organized public relations can bolster democracy by helping leaders be concerned for truth, recognize individuals as important, and behave according to their public pronouncements.

188 Paluszek, John. "Corporate Social Responsibility: PR's Last Big Chance?" *Public Relations Journal* 28 (November 1972): 66.
　　　　Corporations are forming top-level positions to centralize and coordinate social responsibility activities. Although public relations professionals are uniquely qualified for these positions, they are seldom selected to fill them. Given the increasing importance of these top-level management spots, PR practitioners should position themselves to compete for them.

189 Paluszek, John. "Public Relations and Ethical Leadership." *Vital Speeches of the Day,* 1 October 1989, 747-50
　　　　Because PR practitioners "operate at the interface," they play an important ethical leadership role. In political campaign financing and business management, PR can perform an early warning function, refer especially difficult questions to ethics experts, and keep advice simple and practical.

190 Parry, Thomas W. "Public Relations–A Challenge and an Opportunity." *Public Relations Journal* 4 (October 1948): 31-34.

    PR counselors must promote public service because it will lead to public approval and corporate welfare.

191 Parry, Thomas W. "Toward Professional Status for Public Relations." *Public Relations Journal* 5 (July 1949): 10-12.

    To become a socially responsible profession, public relations must require that practitioners have at least a college degree in the liberal arts, that they pass a stiff state certification examination to receive a license, and that they adhere to a code of ethics that has a strong enforcement mechanism.

192 Pearson, Ron. "Albert J. Sullivan's Theory of Public Relations Ethics." *Public Relations Review* 15 (Summer 1989): 52-62.

    Albert J. Sullivan developed the most comprehensive theory of PR ethics. It is the "most complete theory of its kind in the PR literature." Sullivan distinguished technical, partisan, and mutual values in public relations. Because technical values are neither moral nor immoral, PR ethics focuses on the conflict that ensues when partisan and mutual values intersect. Sullivan's theory can be blended with current interest in systems theory to develop a moral as well as a functional basis for PR and to bring added emphasis to current interest in a two-way PR model based on mutuality.

193 Pearson, Ron. "Beyond Ethical Relativism in Public Relations: Coorientation, Rules, and the Idea of Communication Symmetry." In *Public Relations Research Annual* 1, ed. James E. Grunig and Larissa A. Grunig. Hillsdale, N.J.: Erlbaum Associates, 1989, 67-86.

    Coorientation and rules models would afford a useful way to answer questions about communication symmetry, an important issue for PR ethics. Ethical relativism can be avoided by a focus on the structure of interaction between organizations and their publics. The communication environment that promotes dialogue marked by mutual understanding among communicators about the rules in place and mutual satisfaction with these rules is most desirable.

194 Pearson, Ron. "Business Ethics as Communication Ethics: Public Relations Practice and the Idea of Dialogue." In *Public Relations Theory,* ed. Carl H. Botan and Vincent Hazleton, Jr. Hillsdale, N.J.: Lawrence Erlbaum Associates, 1989, 111-31.

    A model of PR ethics based on dialogue is constructed by combining Buchholz's historical concepts of business morality with epistemic assumptions about the nature of knowledge. Within this model, ethics results from negotiations by the organization and its publics. No other source of ethical standard exists. When corporations violate their covenants, the public has grounds to charge them with immoral activity.

195 Pearson, Ron. "Ethical Values or Strategic Values? The Two Faces of Systems Theory in Public Relations." In *Public Relations Research Annual* 2, ed. James Grunig and Larissa Grunig. Hillsdale, N.J.: Lawrence Erlbaum Associates, 1990, 219-34.

    The adoption of systems theory as a framework for PR raises questions about which view of systems will predominate. One view uses systems language to revive management by objectives and functionalism. The other emphasizes collaborative decision making and the ethical implications of interdependence.

196 Pendray, G. Edward, and William W. Cook. "Will We Wait Until We're Cooked?" *Public Relations Journal* 14 (December 1958): 8-12.

    PR is partially responsible for the lack of confidence expressed toward it. PRSA must exert leadership to establish a definition of PR and related terms, hammer out a code of ethics, develop sanctions to reprimand wrongdoers, and develop a PR program for PR.

197 Petzinger, Thomas, Jr. "Crisis PR: When Disaster Comes, Public Relations Men Won't Be Far Behind." *Wall Street Journal,* 23 August 1979, 1, 27.

    When faced with a crisis, most companies employ PR counselors to formulate a disaster plan for dealing with the media and the public. Crisis public relations does not achieve desired results – it may even heighten rather than diminish sensationalism – but presenting the company point of view can minimize negative publicity.

198 "Philippines' Use of U.S. PR Firms Rapped." *Jack O'Dwyer's Newsletter*, 28 June 1989, 7.

    Philippines president Corazon Aquino has been accused of spending $1.44 million on sixteen U.S. public relations and lobbying firms in three years. Some of this PR activity has been linked to the CIA.

199 Plank, Betsy Ann. "The New Technology and Its Implications for the Public Relations Profession." *IPRA Review* 7 (August 1983): 35-38.

    As a responsible profession in the information age, public relations should guide the social changes that new communications technologies will bring about. Such "management of change" requires that new technologies be encouraged, but with safeguards to protect against such technological tyrannies as invasion of privacy, alienation, and inequality.

200 Plumley, Joe, David Ferguson, Scott M. Cutlip, Donald B. McCammond, Melvin L. Sharpe, Frank W. Wylie, Deni Elliott, and H. Scott Hastevold. "Cases and Commentaries." *Journal of Mass Media Ethics* 4, no. 1 (1989): 106-24.

Several persons discuss the case of Anthony Franco, who accepted the presidency of the Public Relations Society of America while he was under investigation by the Securities and Exchange Commission for insider trading and withdrew from PRSA before its Ethics Board could rule on his conduct. Conclusions range from ambivalence to condemnation, most arguing in terms of the negative effect of the Franco affair on PRSA.

201 Pollock, John C. "Business Ethics Affect Bottom Line." *Communication World,* July/August 1989, 48-49.

A survey of six hundred communication and PR professionals indicated that 85 percent think that ethics contributes to corporate profits. About 40 percent believe that their companies are doing more about ethical misconduct than they have done before and most think that management is very concerned about ethics.

202 "Post-Tylenol Crisis Study Finds Public Relations Philosophy Pays Off in Profits, Stock Value . . . Tenfold or More! But Serving the Public Must Be Central to Your Being." *pr reporter*, 30 January 1984, 1-2.

According to a Johnson & Johnson study of fifteen companies that have proclaimed public service as their central mission for at least a generation, public-spirited PR policies have lead to greater profits. In Johnson & Johnson's own case, the company spent $50 million to recall the entire stock of Tylenol after several persons died from adulterated capsules. Despite massive news coverage of the poisonings, the company has since regained 90 percent of its previous sales volume.

203 "PR Groups Combine on Code of Ethics." *Jack O'Dwyer's Newsletter*, 18 May 1988, 2.

A common code of ethics has been accepted by seven of the twelve PR associations who are members of the North American PR Council. PRSA is not one of the twelve, but the issue will be presented for assembly approval in November.

204 Pratt, Catherine A., and Terry Lynn Rentner. "What's Really Being Taught about Ethical Behavior." *Public Relations Review* 15 (Spring 1989): 53-66.

A content analysis of introductory PR textbooks revealed that although all discussed ethics, their terminology and discussion varied. All identified ethics as an individual choice and emphasized its importance. Only *Managing Public Relations* by Grunig and Hunt integrated PR and ethical theory.

205 Pratt, Cornelius B., and Gerald W. McLaughlin. "Ethical Inclinations of Public Relations Majors." *Journal of Mass Media Ethics* 4, no. 1 (1989): 68-91.

A survey of 258 students in PR at two mid-Atlantic public universities indicated that their ethical beliefs were "moderately high." The scale measured four ethical behaviors in five different situations. Students most frequently concurred with "Collegial Support and Normative" behaviors, which are consistent with the "technician" role in PR.

206 Prout, Gerald. "On Expecting Corporate Ethical Reform." *Public Relations Review* 4 (Summer 1978): 13-21.

Despite recent arguments for ethical reform in corporate America, historical and organizational factors are working against the success of such initiatives. The legacy of the Puritans has led to a renouncement of spirit but adherence to economic goals. The concrete language of business is best suited to economic, rather than ethical, discussion. Furthermore, the corporate decision-making process reduces individual accountability, because each decision is cushioned by the organizational structure.

207 "Prout Sees Challenge to Integrity of PR." *Editor & Publisher*, 16 November 1968, 98.

Charles A. Prout, president of the Wisconsin chapter of PRSA, spoke out against those who threaten democracy by distorting the public opinion-making process for their private purposes. Public officials, educators, and the news media are especially responsible for protecting the integrity of information. PR practitioners must disclose their special interests.

208 "PRSA/D.C. May Hold Debate on CIA Ethics Case." *O'Dwyer's PR Services Report,* August 1989, 1, 27-29.

As a result of the ethics case involving four PRSA members who advised CIA head William Casey, PRSA is considering public discussion of the proper role of public relations people in government affairs. The discussion would also cover the Ethics Board's exoneration of the four members as well as the investigation of Summer Harrison, who lodged the initial complaint.

209 "Public Relations Group's Franco Quits in Wake of SEC Case." *Wall Street Journal,* 8 September 1986, 10.
    Anthony M. Franco resigned the presidency of PRSA after the Securities and Exchange Commission made public its allegations that Franco had engaged in insider trading.

210 "Public Relations Society Says Ex-Chief Quits Group." *Wall Street Journal,* 6 October 1986, 15.
    Former PRSA president Anthony M. Franco resigned from PRSA as the society met to determine whether he had violated the Code of Professional Standards.

211 Purcell, Theodore V. "Institutionalizing Ethics into Top Management Decisions." *Public Relations Quarterly* 22 (Summer 1977): 15-20.
    To implement ethical decision making, organizations need an "ethics advocate" to examine general ethical principles, applied or "middle" ethical principles, and in-depth case studies.

212 "The Quietest Revolution." *Public Relations Journal* 18 (March 1962): 18-22.
    President of the British Institute of Public Relations Alan Eden-Green and journalist and critic Malcolm Muggeridge explored the role of PR in a televised debate on BBC-TV in Britain. Key issues included the role of PR in society, the nature of objectivity, falsification of information, and whether PR helps or harms society.

213 "Raymond's CIA Origin Worries Wick." *Jack O'Dwyer's Newsletter,* 16 November 1988, 7.
    The appointment of Walter Raymond, Jr., a former CIA official, as an assistant director of the U.S. Information Agency may hurt the agency's credibility. One PR person said, "It is unfortunate that PR skills have been associated with espionage."

214 Reeves, Byron, and Mary Ann Ferguson-DeThorne. "Measuring the Effect of Messages about Social Responsibility." *Public Relations Review* 6 (Fall 1980): 40-55.
    Three types of social responsibility are profit, the idea that a corporation should maximize profits to further the free market system;

good citizenship, where a corporation participates in activities that promote the public good; and leadership, or the corporate role in solving social problems. A research experiment revealed that the "good citizenship" concept had the greatest positive effect on subjects' attitudes toward corporations.

215 Ross, Irwin. *The Image Merchants: The Fabulous World of Public Relations.* Garden City, N.Y.: Doubleday, 1959.

Public relations, "the pursuit of public approval through the merchandising of favorable impressions of the client," is seeking the aura of professionalism to raise its status and impress clients. Under the guise of public interest, PR tries to sell the merits of a particular corporation and the merits of contemporary American capitalism. Public relations is an inevitable outgrowth of a complex society. Communications have become so cumbersome that an institution must use an intricate set of tools to make effective contact with its publics. Public relations is even beneficial: businesses are much more forthcoming than they used to be, and they exercise enlightened self-interest in terms of community support and philanthropy.

Junkets and other means of courting favor, however, create a conflict of interest that hinders the proper function of news media. Moreover, public relations often inhibits a free flow of information by obfuscation, distraction, and the promotion of half-truths. To counter the negative aspects of PR, news media should systematically resist the largesse of PR professionals and report the public relations activity behind every significant news story.

216 Rothenberg, Randall. "Playing the B-Roll Bop." *The Quill,* September 1990, 27-31.

To control their image on television news, corporations are using video news releases. Between five and fifteen thousand VNRs are produced and distributed annually, and 70 percent of television stations are willing to use them in their news broadcasts. Not only are VNRs far less expensive than broadcast advertisements, but seen on the news they are more credible, an important consideration given that more than half of the adults in the United States rely on television for news.

217 Rowe, Kenneth, and John Schlacter. "Integrating Social Responsibility into the Corporate Structure." *Public Relations Quarterly* 23 (Fall 1978): 7-12.

Many firms committed to the idea of social responsibility lack concrete guidelines that tell them how to proceed. They must first establish specific objectives that are compatible with corporate goals and can be achieved within a specific time frame. Second, they must develop concrete plans of action, which often require changing the corporate structure to accommodate new objectives and gathering information about social or environmental impact. Finally, results of the program must be evaluated and incentives to continue socially responsible activities must be provided.

218 Rubin, Maureen Shubow. "VNRs: Re-Examining 'Unrestricted Use.'" *Public Relations Journal* 45 (October 1989): 58-60.

There is no evidence that video news releases (VNRs) have been misused, but because there are no legal safeguards, stations can legally use the tapes for purposes very different from what the client intended. VNRs should be accompanied by a statement that restricts use and warns stations that legal action may be taken for violations.

219 Rushford, Greg. "PR Group in Ethics Tussle over CIA Advice." *Legal Times,* 12 June 1989, 1, 12-13.

Controversy within the PRSA is creating negative publicity for that group. The controversy centers on the PRSA Ethics Board's decision that four public relations people who advised CIA head William Casey did not violate the society's ethical guidelines. Summer Harrison, who filed the complaint, was then accused of violating the code because she did not keep her concerns about PR members advising government officials confidential. If Harrison is expelled from PRSA, the managing director of Hill and Knowlton, who does not belong to PRSA, has threatened to organize a "Free Summer Harrison Committee" and mount a PR campaign against the association.

220 Ryan, Michael. "Public Relations Practitioners' Views of Corporate Social Responsibility." *Journalism Quarterly* 63 (Winter 1986): 740-47, 762.

To fulfill their ethical roles in corporations, PR practitioners must be committed to corporate social responsibility. Survey results indicate that most PR people are committed, but a substantial minority are not. Inconsistency between answers to some survey questions suggests that practitioners may not act the way they say they would.

221 Ryan, Michael, and David L. Martinson. "Ethical Values, the Flow of Journalistic Information and Public Relations Persons." *Journalism Quarterly* 61 (Spring 1984): 27-34.

A survey sent to 260 members of the PRSA asked for responses to hypothetical situations. Results confirm that practitioners are guided by ethical relativism. In cases involving great risk to the public, practitioners want to disclose all information. They are more likely to cover things up if few people are involved and if the decision does not affect the public. PR practitioners try to balance the needs of the client with the needs of the public. Most practitioners see themselves as morally responsible for their actions, but they experience great stress when attempting to solve moral dilemmas. Guidelines that apply to all areas of PR need to be established.

222 Ryan, Michael, and David L. Martinson. "Exercise Helps Students to Judge Ethics Choices Made by PR Professionals." *Public Relations Research & Education* 2 (1985): 48-52.
    Students are asked to respond to two hypothetical examples–one regarding the firing of an athletic coach, the other regarding a medical research laboratory's disposal of nuclear waste–and their responses are discussed in light of those that PR practitioners gave in a national survey.

223 Ryan, Michael, and David L. Martinson. "The PR Officer as Corporate Conscience." *Public Relations Quarterly* 28 (Summer 1983): 20-23.
    PR officers, who are often employed in the highest levels of corporations, should maintain their independence so they do not become so entrenched into top management that they are no longer effective, and they should be the corporate conscience, responsible to a morality higher than management authority. Because the PR person is uniquely qualified to fulfill these responsibilities, corporations must allow PR people to collect information, attend meetings, and argue against decisions without fear of repercussions. No one person is always right, however, so PR officers should be willing to bend to corporate dictates unless the public's welfare is threatened.

224 Ryan, Michael, and David L. Martinson. "Public Relations Practitioners, Public Interest and Management." *Journalism Quarterly* 62 (Spring 1985): 111-15.
    A survey of 260 PR people indicated that they do not want management to define the PR role, they will not implement management policies if they are not in the public interest, and they want to work with management to change policies that are not in the best interests of the public. Most also agreed that PR persons are as concerned as journalists about getting complete, accurate information to the public. A minority of practitioners indicated little concern for the public interest. Controlling those practitioners is still required.

225 Schuyler, Philip N. "Dean of PR Seeks to Raise Craft Level." *Editor & Publisher*, 27 February 1960, 26.

Harry A. Bruno, president of H. A. Bruno Associates, advocates licensing tests for admission into the practice of public relations. He opposes the use of "fronts," by which organizations pursue an undisclosed agenda under the guise of a different announced purpose. Licensing tests would diminish such practices by testing judgment as well as technique.

226 "S.E.C. Accuses P.R. Executive." *New York Times*, 27 August 1986, D3.

The Securities and Exchange Commission accused PRSA president Anthony M. Franco of insider trading.

227 Seligman, Mac. "Travel Writers' Expenses: Who Should Pay?" *Public Relations Journal* 46 (May 1990): 27-28, 34.

Although many newspapers and magazines oppose host-subsidized travel for writers on the grounds that it will bias the stories, sponsorship need not compromise a writer's prose. PR firms desire fair, balanced travel stories, just as the media do. Travel subsidies enable underfunded travel writers to visit various destinations, and they ensure that the media have fresh stories.

228 Shaffer, W. M. "Hope Springs Eternal for Good Use of PR." *Marketing News*, 25 September 1989, 1-2.

Although PR should be in a golden era, its lack of professional, results-oriented practices keeps it on the margins of marketing. PR agencies measure themselves according to billing hours rather than measurable success in the market. Such measurable success can be determined by answering six questions: Did the product sell? Did the promotion work? Did opinion change? Did attitudes move? Did stock prices rise? Did executive visibility increase?

229 Sharpe, Melvin L. "The Professional Need: Standards for the Performance of Public Relations." *IPRA Review* 10 (November 1986): 10-16.

In order to demonstrate to organizations, the press, and the public that public relations is a profession with a strong sense of social responsibility, it must follow standards by which clients are willing to abide. Acceptable standards for organizational public relations would clearly state the need for organizations to have both published ethics and published communications policies, the precise ways they will employ and use PR professionals, and the need for two-way communication between organizations and their publics.

230 "Should We 'Engineer' People's Minds?" *Public Relations Journal* 4 (April 1957): 2, 24.

Public relations should provide information openly for the public to consider; it should not use "fronts" or other surreptitious means to create public opinion. One is forthright and democratic; the other is cynical and manipulative.

231 Simon, Julie. "How to Handle Travel and Tourism Freebies." *Public Relations Journal* 44 (June 1988): 33-34.

Although large publications like the *Wall Street Journal*, the *New York Times*, and Conde Nast's *Traveler* reject travel freebies, many media outlets and free-lance writers accept them because they cannot cover travel stories otherwise. To avoid misunderstandings, PR representatives should communicate clearly with the press regarding mutual responsibilities when arranging free trips. They may ask for clippings but not for favorable coverage, for example, and they should specify the extent of their hospitality (e.g., for reporters but not for reporters' guests, for meals but not for room-service drinks).

232 Smith, Allen N. "The Principle of Advocacy." *Public Relations Quarterly* 17 (Summer 1972): 9-11, 23-24.

Public relations is like law in that an agent is loyal to the client, the agent and client are honest with each other, and the agent presents the best face of the client to the public. Lies backfire, so that although the PR agent is selective about what information to share, the information should always be accurate.

233 Smith, Rea W. "Commentary on Code of Ethics of Public Relations Society of America." In *The Ethical Basis of Economic Freedom*, ed. Ivan Hill. Chapel Hill: American Viewpoint, 1976, 283-90.

Five years after the Public Relations Society of America was formed in 1947, it adopted its first Code of Ethics, a code that has been revised for specificity and enforcement procedures and that has gathered a large body of interpretation since its adoption. The PRSA maintains that a voluntary code is better than state licensing, which would add burdensome red tape and threaten freedom of expression without enhancing integrity. The code will continue to gain authority as more and more public relations professionals become members of the PRSA.

234 "Society Gets Code to Judge Members." *Editor & Publisher*, 23 January 1960, 54.

The PRSA revised its Code of Professional Conduct, expanding the issues it covers and modifying its enforcement procedures.

235 "The Speakes Case: Where the Field Went Wrong." *Public Relations Journal* 45 (February 1989): 39-40.

Although White House press spokesman Larry Speakes told reporters that he wanted his epitaph to read, "He told the truth . . . always," Speakes admitted later that he manufactured quotations for President Reagan. Two such quotations that Speakes supplied the press followed the Geneva summit with Gorbachev. Reporters were told that Reagan said to Gorbachev, "There is much that divides us, but I believe the world breathes easier because we are talking here together," and, "Our differences are serious, but so is our commitment to improving understanding." Instead of rallying behind the concept of trust, PR practitioners gave a divided evaluation of Speakes's admission.

236 Speck, Bruce W. "Ethics: A Bridge for Studying the Social Contexts of Professional Communication." *Journal of Business and Technical Communication* 3 (January 1989): 70-88.

Teachers of professional communication have the responsibility of addressing moral issues in the classroom. Kohlberg's theory is particularly suited to this task because it addresses motivation. Applying Kohlberg's theory to case studies in professional communication raises students' awareness of the need for careful ethical deliberation.

237 Spikol, Art. "Collision Course." *Writer's Digest,* October 1980, 8, 10-11.

Free-lance writers face a conflict of interest when they are asked by a business to write a promotional article under their byline for an independent magazine. Writers should be scrupulously honest about content and payment with both the business and the publisher, and they should consider ghostwriting the article for management. Writers should never compromise their integrity or their good name.

238 Spitzer, Carlton E. "Case for the Honest Ghost." *Public Relations Journal* 19 (November 1963): 11-12, 14.

Ghostwriting is not the mercenary practice that some critics claim; rather, it is often necessary and honorable in both government and business.

239 Spitzer, Carlton E. "The High Price of Popularity." *Public Relations Journal* 18 (January 1962): 14-15.

Public relations can earn respect in the long run by being objective and by avoiding the temptation simply to appease majority corporate interest.

240 Spitzer, Carlton E. "Should Government Audit Corporate Social Responsibility?" *Public Relations Review* 7 (Summer 1981): 13-28.

To avoid increased government regulation, corporations need to take initiatives that help solve social problems. Business and government should work in tandem.

241 Stacks, Don W., and Donald K. Wright. "A Quantitative Examination of Ethical Dilemmas in Public Relations." *Journal of Mass Media Ethics* 4, no. 1 (1989): 53-67.

A survey of 109 communication students suggests that students and PR practitioners share responses to selected moral quandaries.

242 Stephenson, D. R. "Internal PR Efforts Further Corporate Responsibility: A Report from Dow Canada." *Public Relations Quarterly* 28 (Summer 1983): 7-10.

PR efforts will have little impact unless management understands that solving social problems is both good business and good citizenship. To change management's attitudes toward social responsibility and the function of public relations, Dow Chemical in Canada circulated a booklet of quotations representing Dow's operational philosophies, and it trained top executives and managers in dealing with the media.

243 Steumpfle, Herman G. "Public Relations Executives." In *On-the-Job Ethics: A Pioneering Analysis by Men Engaged in Six Major Occupations,* ed. Cameron P. Hall. New York: National Council of the Churches of Christ in the U.S.A., 1963, 93-96.

The Department of the Church and Economic Life of the National Council of Churches organized a series of ten luncheons with nineteen public relations professions from a variety of institutions. They discussed ethical issues and cases concerning the role of the PR practitioner, truth, and personal integrity. Six months later, the group met again to discuss how to involve a wider body of public relations professionals in the serious ethical dialogue in which the group was engaged.

244 Steward, Hal D. "It's What You Do That Counts." *Public Relations Quarterly* 3 (April 1958): 18-24.

PR associations must take responsibility for moral and ethical matters in intraprofessional relationships, client relationships, and relationships with the public. Associations need to state their aims and responsibilities, list improper practices and conduct; establish warning procedures for violators, expel any member who is found guilty of unethical conduct, and develop and execute a public information program to explain the positive values of public relations.

245 Stillman, Charles C. "Ethical Standards in Social Work Publicity." *Hospital Social Service* 21 (January 1930): 23-29.

The result for the public, not the client, must be the yardstick used to measure ethical social work publicity. Publicity should be undertaken only when the issues are important enough to justify the time and money spent and when it can be intelligently used to pursue worthy ends.

246 Sullivan, Albert J. "Value Systems of Public Relations." *Public Relations Quarterly* 8 (Winter 1963): 5-12.

The first in a series of three essays on public relations values focuses on technique, which is measured by efficiency and economy rather than by moral criteria. Strategy, creation, and production are the elements of public relations technique. Although its creation and production are by and large competent, public relations flounders strategically because its campaigns are based more on intuition than on science.

247 Sullivan, Albert J. "The Value Systems of Public Relations, II." *Public Relations Quarterly* 8 (July 1963): 15-25.

The second in a series of three essays on public relations values focuses on partisanship–one's commitment, trust, loyalty, and obedience to the institution being promoted. Although usually praiseworthy, unbridled partisanship can lead to deceit and injustice. Public relations practitioners should beware of blind faith, winning at all cost, and opposition to dialogue.

248 Sullivan, Albert J. "The Value Systems of Public Relations, III." *Public Relations Quarterly* 8 (October 1963): 28-40.

The third in a series of three essays on public relations values focuses on two human rights: the right to true information and the right to participate in decisions concerning all matters of relevance. Only by ensuring free discussion with true information as a matter of respect for all persons can public relations find its raison d'être as a profession.

249 Sullivan, Frank C. "The Dimensions of Disbelief." *Public Relations Quarterly* 23 (Spring 1978): 25-27.

To overcome public distrust and to ensure the survival of business, decisions must be based on public interest, integrity, and truth.

250 Summar, Dwayne, and R. Keith Moore. "Lying Is Professional Suicide." *Wall Street Journal,* 30 July 1987, 23.

Two letters to the editor object to a claim made by Matt Zachowski, president of Nycom Associates, a New York public relations and marketing firm, that "if Col. North is lying he's lying very well, which would make him a highly excellent PR guy." Truth is a key to the PRSA Code of Professional Practices; as all PR professionals know, lying destroys credibility.

251 "Survey Shows Need of Ethics Code for Newsmen Dealing with PR People, Wylie Tells AP Managing Editors Association." *pr reporter,* 10 December 1973, 1-2.

Because of continued ethical transgressions by newspeople, the Associated Press Managing Editors Association should develop a code of conduct to guide transactions between the press and public relations. According to results of a survey conducted by Frank Wylie, PR manager for Chrysler Corporation, newspeople often ask PR people for special favors, offer them combined advertising and editorial space, and participate in junkets. Newspeople rarely check their stories with sources for verification of facts and increasingly report sensational stories where "made-up facts are common."

252 Thau, Theadore L. "A Call for Action." *PR in Canada* 6 (February 1963): 12-15.

To promote public confidence in business and to maintain the free enterprise system, public relations professionals should help businesses attain high ethical standards.

253 "Town Won't Return HUD Funds Used for PR." *Jack O'Dwyer's Newsletter,* 26 July 1989, 2.

The Department of Housing and Urban Development seeks the return of $95,728 that the village of Hempstead in Long Island, New York, paid to Paul Townsend, chairman of Townsend Communications and editor of *Long Island Business News.* HUD opposes paying two PR firms simultaneously: Townsend Communications and the defunct Columbia Images.

254 Traverse-Healy, Tim. "Public Relations and Propaganda Values Compared." *IPRA Review* 12, no. 1 (1988): 29-30.
The PR calling involves understanding interdependence, managing information disclosure, and balancing conflicting interests. Expertise is not sufficient to perform these socially significant tasks successfully: public trust is crucial. Because trust will come only by establishing a record of concern, honesty, and fair consultation, practitioners' actions must be policed and the definition of public interest should be debated.

255 Tretbar, Everett E. "Beware the Phony PR Pitchman!" *Industrial Marketing,* March 1959, 152.
Too many PR practitioners promise national media exposure that never materializes. Such trading on sales managers' gullibility hurts the honest PR agent, whose steady, if unglamorous, work can improve market penetration.

256 Urrows, Henry H. "Ethics for a New Profession." *Public Relations Journal* 5 (February 1949): 9-10.
To be accepted as a profession, PR needs a code of ethics. Because of divergent perspectives, developing such a code will involve conflict.

257 van der Meiden, Anne. "Public Relations, the Netherlands and Ethics–A Meditative and Critical Analysis." *IPRA Review* 9 (November 1985): 11-13.
Publicity concerning hypocrisy in the professions since the 1950s has led to the devaluation of universal moral principles in favor of a "morality of the feasible." Ethics has grown individualistic, emphasizing the ability to live with one's decisions over the ability to gain the acceptance of others. The present need in communication ethics is for a record of the solutions that professionals have implemented in actual situations. This casuistry requires an answer to the question, what is the essential difference between communication professions? The answer to this question requires empirical data on the criteria that practitioners of different communication professions use in their decision making.

258 Van Leuven, James K. "Measuring Values through Public Participation." *Public Relations Review* 6 (Spring 1980): 51-56.
Personal value inventories, which can help assess the degree of value congruence between interest groups and agencies, are important because public involvement is desirable–sometimes even legally

mandated – for public policy making. A personal value inventory used to compare personal value hierarchies of nine interest groups involved in planning under the National Wild and Scenic River Program revealed that environmentalists differed more from the composite profile than did any other single group. Users and conservationists differed significantly on certain other key issues.

259 Walsh, Frank. "Practitioners' Role in Releasing Market-Sensitive Information." *Public Relations Journal* 40 (May 1984): 32-33.

Financial PR practitioners are required both legally and by the PRSA code to know SEC rules and regulations. PR practitioners must be objective in the release of market-sensitive information.

260 Warmer, George A. "Public Relations and Privacy." In *Information, Influence, & Communication: A Reader in Public Relations,* ed. Otto Lerginger and Albert J. Sullivan. New York: Basic Books, 1965, 440-65. Reprinted from George A. Warmer, "Public Relations and Privacy," *College and University Journal* 2, no. 4 (1964), 33-38.

PR is at the center of the conflict between the individual's right to know and his or her right to privacy. Although PR disseminates true information to concerned publics, those who do not need or want the information are also reached. Misinformation tends to exploit rather than to inform, and potentially manipulative messages deny the freedom to know all of the truth and make an individual decision.

Because there are few laws restricting the right to disseminate information, moral insight or courtesy must direct PR decisions. Existing codes reflect a need for status rather than essential integrity.

Because moral and immoral people have the same access to PR techniques and psychological-social insights and because the professional task of PR is potentially more profound than that of other professions, the standards of public relations practitioners must continue to rise.

261 Watson, Bruce. "Whither the Society's Code?" *Public Relations Journal* 16 (October 1960): 23-26.

Members of the Public Relations Society of America are obliged to follow the Code of Professional Standards. The code is hortatory, so it is up to the membership to make the code come alive and it is up to the National Judicial Council to interpret the code on a case-by-case basis when disputes arise.

262 Watson, Campbell. "PR Society Sets Up Accrediting Program." *Editor & Publisher*, 23 November 1963, 13.

A new accreditation program to elevate standards for PR practice was approved by PRSA's Board of Delegates. All PRSA members who have eight years of PR experience are eligible to take the qualifying examinations for accreditation. Additionally, the ninety-member board accepted the Committee on Standards guide for interpreting the Code of Professional Standards section regarding financial PR. It also elected new officers.

263 Weaver, Paul H. "Evade, Obscure, Fudge." *Business Month,* April 1988, 63-67.

A former Ford Motor Company executive explains how the truth was irrelevant in corporate communications regarding Ford's decision to manufacture V-6 engines in Windsor, Ontario, rather than in Lima, Ohio.

264 Weiss, E. B. "Public Relations or Public Roadblocks – Which Is the More Accurate Description?" *Advertising Age,* 21 December 1964, 34.

Public relations practitioners are often loath to disclose information, even information that could be easily obtained by examining public documents. Silence achieves nothing because secrecy cannot be maintained, and it is unnecessary.

265 Weiss, E. B. "The 'Unpublic' Relations of Public Relations." *Advertising Age,* 16 October 1967, 98-100.

Public relations is ill equipped to counsel clients on the new social order because practitioners do not understand social responsibility or the range of problems facing business today.

266 Wilcox, Dennis L. "Criticism, Evaluation and Professionalism." *Public Relations Journal* 35 (November 1979): 56-57.

The PR profession needs "insightful, critical analysis" and practitioners should speak up if they see instances of incompetent behavior, especially if the incident is already the object of media scrutiny. Although the Code of Professional Standards states that a practitioner may not intentionally act to hurt another, professionals can criticize when doing so is in the best interest of the profession and the public.

267 Wilcox, Dennis L., and Sydney C. Avey. *Ethics and Candor in Public Relations and Organizational Communication: A Literature Review.* San Francisco: IABC Foundation, 1984.

This annotated bibliography lists nearly two hundred sources on advertising ethics, business ethics, codes of conduct, communicator ethics, mass media ethics, occupational standards, personal ethics, philosophy of ethics, and teaching of ethics written between 1974 and mid-1984. An essay at the end summarizes key themes and recommends sixteen areas for research.

268 Winkleman, Michael. "On the Air." *Public Relations Journal* 43 (July 1987): 2.

Concerns about identification of the source of video news releases (VNRs) are addressed in the PRSA code, which states that the identity of the client or employer must be available to the public. The responsibility for disclosing the source then rests with editors. The ethics code that guides professional journalists does not clearly stipulate how to handle VNRs.

269 Winkleman, Michael. "Soul Searching." *Public Relations Journal* 43 (October 1987): 28-32.

The increased emphasis on ethics has led to concern about the PR profession itself. Seminars offered by professional organizations, the attention given to codes, and the strengthening of sanctions for code violations have increased awareness of corporate codes and enhanced clients' reputations. The soul-searching that has accompanied the ethical crisis will define PR's role in the future.

270 Winks, Donald. "Speaking Out–With a Forked Tongue." *Business Week*, 2 July 1979, 9.

To regain public trust, executives must talk to the public the way they talk to each other. Their failure to do this has led to mistrust and the loss of public goodwill.

271 Wood, Robert J. "What the Public Expects of Business." *Public Relations Journal* 26 (October 1970): 22-24, 128.

Expecting business to solve all social ills is overoptimistic. Although many corporations are engaged in responsible community activities, solid public relations programs must be designed to cushion public disappointment when business is unable to do everything that is expected of it.

272 Wright, Donald K. "Age and the Moral Values of Practitioners." *Public Relations Review* 11 (Spring 1985): 51-60.

Measuring fifty moral behaviors using a Likert-type scale revealed that PR practitioners have "moderate" to "high" levels of conventional morality. In general, older practitioners scored higher on basic morality and basic honesty, but did not statistically differ from younger practitioners in terms of economic morality, religious morality, and legal issues.

273 Wright, Donald K. "Analysis of Ethical Principles among Canadian Public Relations Practitioners." *IPRA Review* 9 (May 1985): 23-29.

Ethical decisions ultimately rest with individual practitioners. A survey measuring the moral beliefs of 104 members of two Canadian IABC chapters revealed a "moderate to high" level of moral and ethical values. The highest levels of ethical thought were found in response to items measuring basic human morality and economic morality, and women exhibited higher moral judgments than did men.

274 Wright, Donald K. "Ethics in Public Relations." *Public Relations Journal* 38 (December 1982): 12, 14-16.

The public demands higher moral standards, and PR societies have instituted codes of professional standards to guide members' behavior. Empirical research needs to be conducted to move PR from ethical relativism to a morality based on justice, equality, and individual human dignity.

275 Wright, Donald K. "Examining Ethical and Moral Values of Public Relations People." *Public Relations Review* 2 (Summer 1989): 19-33.

Public relations as a profession is no more ethical than are the people who practice it. A factor analysis of a fifty-item Likert-type scale completed by 424 American and Canadian IABC members and students in university PR classes suggests that moral values can be measured and differentiated into six categories: socioeconomic morality, religious morality, basic morality, puritanical morality, basic social responsibility morality, and financial morality.

276 Wright, Donald K. "Individual Ethics Determine Public Relations Practice." *Public Relations Journal* 41 (April 1985): 38-39.

Despite recurring public statements that "All PR people are flacks and liars," research has shown that there are no moral differences between PR practitioners and others. PR people should assert this when told that their profession is unethical.

277 Wright, Donald K. "Moral Values and Ethics." *IPRA Review* 9 (November 1985): 14-17.

Ten years of social science research suggests that moral responsibility is a matter of individual choice. Although results vary by sex, age, and length of time in the field, research suggests that most PR people are socially responsible.

Because some unethical and immoral people practice PR, public relations needs licensing or registration for practitioners, or at least an enforceable code. Practitioners must prevent the "fraudulent" misuse of the term "public relations" and publicly defend the field when it is accused of irresponsibility. Finally, PR education and research must be supported.

278 Wright, Donald K. "The Philosophy of Ethical Development in Public Relations." *IPRA Review* 6 (April 1982): 22-27.

The ethical relativism that characterizes public relations is outdated; PR needs to advance to a stage that recognizes justice, equality, and human dignity as moral universals.

279 Wright, Donald K. "Professionalism and Social Responsibility in Public Relations." *Public Relations Review* 5 (Fall 1979): 20-33.

Because PR is a unique field, debates about its professionalism or social responsibility cannot be resolved. The professionalism and orientations toward social responsibility of individual PR practitioners can be assessed, however. A survey of PR practitioners in Texas indicated great variation in levels of professionalism and degree of orientation toward social responsibility. Although few PR people indicated that they were both highly professional and highly concerned with social responsibility, many said they want to be more professional and socially responsible than their jobs allow them to be. Most agreed that there should be regulation by peers, that PR education should be encouraged, and that the field should be altruistic, but also indicated that PR lacks a broad range of autonomy and an enforceable code of ethics.

280 Wright, Donald K. "Social Responsibility in Public Relations: A Multi-Step Theory." *Public Relations Review* 2 (Fall 1976): 24-36.

Interviews with PR practitioners suggest that social responsibility increases when respect from management is high and degree of supervision low, and when practitioners have an active role in corporate decision making and full professional status.

281 Wylie, Frank W. "A Common Code of Ethics." *Public Relations Journal* 30 (February 1974): 14-15.

A survey of PRSA members indicated that journalists and PR practitioners share ethical concerns. The two groups should work together on a common code of ethics, enforce the ethical policies that have been defined, and banish persistent violators from both fields.

282 Wylie, Frank W. "Ethics in College and University Public Relations." *Public Relations Review* 15 (Summer 1989): 63-67.

Results of a survey of university PR directors, presidents, and local media representatives suggest that university presidents should increase the pay and status of PR directors to attract persons with great experience and talent. These experienced practitioners should be trusted to determine newsworthiness of releases. University presidents should also allocate funds for professional development of PR directors, and increase awareness of truth and accuracy requirements; they should not ask PR practitioners to intercede with the college newspaper.

283 Wylie, Frank W., and Barbara D. Langham. "Ethics: Where Do You Stand?" *Communication World* 6 (May 1989): 21-25.

A survey answered by 151 persons involved in college public relations indicates varying levels of confidence in the information that colleges and universities release. College presidents unanimously say that the information their colleges release is accurate and not misleading, and 86 percent of local media professionals agree. However, 72 percent of college public relations professionals express complete confidence in enrollment data, 61 percent in fund-raising information, and 55 percent in information regarding athletics.

284 "Yet More Vituperation on the Profession." *pr reporter*, 13 May 1985, 2.

Albert Abend of Aetna complains that Marvin Olasky is giving public relations erroneous bad publicity. According to Abend, Olasky believes in one truth, which PR violates, whereas PR actually is involved in the negotiation of various perspectives.

285 Young, Davis. "We Are in the Business of Enhancing Trust." *Public Relations Journal* 42 (January 1986): 7-8.

To meet their ethical responsibility, PR practitioners must realize that PR is a business practiced with professional standards, not a profession, recognize that PR must strive to be accountable for results, emphasize full disclosure, promote substance rather than technique, avoid impropriety, strive for professional status much like that which auditing firms command, and advance individual development.

Appendix: Public Relations Society of America's Codes of Professional Standards

PROFESSIONAL STANDARDS

FOR THE PRACTICE

OF PUBLIC RELATIONS

As members of the Public Relations Society of America, we subscribe to the belief that inherent in the practice of public relations is the obligation of a public trust which requires fulfillment of these principles:

1. Objectives which are in full accord with the public welfare as well as the interests of our clients or employers;

2. Accuracy, truthfulness, and good taste in material prepared for public dissemination and in all other activities sponsored, participated in or promoted, whether as independent public relations counsel or as officer or employee of a trade association, company or other organization or group;

3. Standards of practice which preclude the serving of competitors concurrently except with the full knowledge and consent of all concerned; which safeguard the confidential affairs of client or employer even after termination of professional association with him and so long as his interests demand; and which, with full regard for our right to profit and to

advance our personal interests, nevertheless preserve professional integrity as the primary concern in our work;

4.   Cooperation with fellow practitioners in curbing malpractice such as the circulation of slanderous statements or rumors, the concealment from clients or employers of discounts or commissions, or any other information to which they are entitled; and deliberate distortion or misrepresentation for professional gain or competitive advantage;

5.   Support of efforts designed to further the ethics and technical proficiency of the profession and encourage the establishment of adequate training and education for the practice of public relations.

We realize full well that interpretation of a Code of Ethics becomes a matter of personal judgment in many instances, but we hold that a sincere effort to implement the spirit of the above principles will assure professional conduct of credit to the profession and honest service to clients and employers.

Adopted by the membership December 4, 1950

PROFESSIONAL STANDARDS

FOR THE PRACTICE

OF PUBLIC RELATIONS

As members of the *Public Relations Society of America,* we share a responsibility for the good character and reputation of the public relations profession. Therefore we pledge ourselves to make a sincere effort to adhere to the following principles and standards of practice:

1. We will keep our objectives in full accord with the public welfare as well as the interests of our clients or employers.

2. We will be guided in all our activities by the standards of accuracy, truth, and good taste.

3. We will safeguard the confidence of both present and former clients or employers.

4. We will not engage in any activity in which we are directly or indirectly in competition with a present client or employer without the full knowledge and consent of all concerned.

5. We will cooperate with fellow practitioners in curbing malpractice.

6. We will support efforts designed to further the technical proficiency of the profession and encourage the establishment of adequate training and education for the practice of public relations.

To the extent that we live up to these principles and standards of practice, we will be meeting our responsibilities for making the profession in which we are engaged worthy of continued public confidence.

> *Reviewed by the Board of Directors of the Public Relations Society of America, at the St. Louis Board Meeting, October 15-16, 1954*

DECLARATION OF PRINCIPLES

Members of the Public Relations Society of America acknowledge and publicly declare that the public relations profession in serving the legitimate interests of clients or employers is dedicated fundamentally to the goals of better mutual understanding and cooperation among the diverse individuals, groups, institutions and elements of our modern society.

In the performance of this mission, we pledge ourselves:

1. To conduct ourselves both privately and professionally in accord with the public welfare.

2. To be guided in all our activities by the generally accepted standards of truth, accuracy, fair dealing and good taste.

3. To support efforts designed to increase the proficiency of the profession by encouraging the continuous development of sound training and resourceful education in the practice of public relations.

4. To adhere faithfully to provisions of the duly adopted Code of Professional Standards for the Practice of Public Relations, a copy of which is in the possession of every member.

Code of Professional Standards
for the Practice of Public Relations

This Code of Professional Standards for the Practice of Public Relations is adopted by the Public Relations Society of America to promote and maintain high standards of public service and conduct among its members in order that membership in the Society may be deemed a badge of ethical conduct; that Public Relations justly may be regarded as a profession; that the public may have increasing confidence in its integrity; and that the practice of Public Relations may best serve the public interest.

1. A member has a general duty of fair dealing towards his clients or employers, past and present, his fellow members and the general public.

2. A member shall conduct his professional life in accord with the public welfare.

3. A member has the affirmative duty of adhering to generally accepted standards of accuracy, truth and good taste.

4.   A member shall not represent conflicting or competing interests without the express consent of those concerned, given after a full disclosure of the facts.

5.   A member shall safeguard the confidences of both present and former clients or employers and shall not accept retainers or employment which may involve the disclosure or use of these confidences to the disadvantage or prejudice of such clients or employers.

6.   A member shall not engage in any practice which tends to corrupt the integrity of channels of public communication.

7.   A member shall not intentionally disseminate false or misleading information and is obligated to use ordinary care to avoid dissemination of false or misleading information.

8.   A member shall not make use of any organization purporting to serve some announced cause but actually serving an undisclosed special or private interest of a member or his client or his employer.

9.   A member shall not intentionally injure the professional reputation or practice of another member. However, if a member has evidence that another member has been guilty of unethical, illegal or unfair practices, including practices in violation of this Code, he should present the information to the proper authorities of the Society for action in accordance with the procedure set forth in Article XIII of the Bylaws.

10.   A member shall not employ methods tending to be derogatory of another member's client or employer or of the products, business or services of such client or employer.

11.   In performing services for a client or employer a member shall not accept fees, commissions or any other valuable consideration in connection with those services from anyone other than his client or employer without the express consent of his client or employer, given after full disclosure of the facts.

12.   A member shall not propose to a prospective client or employer that his fee or other compensation be contingent on the achievement of certain results; nor shall he enter into any fee agreement to the same effect.

13.   A member shall not encroach upon the professional employment of another member unless both are assured that there is no conflict between the two engagements and are kept advised of the negotiations.

14.   A member shall, as soon as possible, sever his relations with any organization when he believes his continued employment would require him to conduct himself contrary to the principles of this Code.

15.   A member called as a witness in a proceeding for the enforcement of this Code shall be bound to appear unless, for sufficient reason, he shall be excused by the panel hearing the same.

16. A member shall co-operate with fellow members in upholding and enforcing this Code.

Adopted in November 1959 by the 1959 PRSA Board of Directors and ratified by the 1960 PRSA Assembly

An Official Interpretation of the PRSA Code of
Professional Standards for the Practice of Public Relations
Applies to Financial Public Relations

1. It is the responsibility of the member practicing financial public relations to know and understand the rules and regulations of the SEC and the laws which it administers and the other laws, rules and regulations affecting financial public relations and to act in accordance with their letter and spirit. (See paragraph 2 of the Code.)

2. It shall be the objective of such member to follow the policy of full disclosure of corporate information, except in such instances where such information is of a confidential nature. The purpose of this objective is to enable an accurate evaluation of the company by the investing public and not to influence the price of securities. Such information should be accurate, clear and understandable. (See paragraphs 1 and 2 of the Code.)

3. Such member shall observe the confidential nature of certain of the information he has access to because of his employment and shall take every precaution to make sure this information is not used in a manner detrimental to his client's or employer's best interests. (See paragraph 5 of the Code.)

4. Such members shall disclose or release information promptly so as to avoid the possibility of any use of the information by an insider for personal gain. In general, such member should make every effort to comply with the spirit and intent of the "Timely Disclosure" provisions of the New York Stock Exchange Company Manual. Information deemed not confidential but which is not subject to a formal release shall be available to all on an equal basis. (See paragraphs 1 and 2 of the Code.)

5. Such member shall exercise reasonable care to ascertain the facts correctly and to disseminate only information which he believes to be accurate and adequate. Such member shall use reasonable care to avoid the issuance or release of predictions or projections of financial or other matters lacking adequate basis in fact. (See paragraph 7 of the Code.)

6. Such member shall act promptly to correct false or misleading information or rumors concerning his client's or employer's securities or business whenever he has reason to believe such information or rumors exist. (See paragraphs 1, 2 and 7 of the Code.)

7. Such member shall clearly identify to the investing public the sources of any communication for which he is responsible, including the name of the client or employer on whose behalf the communication is made. (See paragraph 8 of the Code.)

8. Such member shall not exploit the information he has gained as an insider for personal gain. However, this is not intended to prohibit a member from making bona fide investments in his company's or client's securities in accordance with normal investment practices. (See paragraphs 1 and 4 of the Code.)

9. Such member shall not accept compensation which would place him in a position of conflict with his duty to his client, employer or the investing public. Specifically, such member shall not accept a contingent fee or a stock option from his client or employer unless part of an overall plan in favor of corporate executives, nor shall he accept securities as compensation at a value substantially below market price. (See paragraph 4 of the Code.)

10. Such member shall so act as to maintain the integrity of channels of public communication and to observe generally accepted standards of good taste. He shall as a minimum observe the publicly announced standards published by organizations representing the media of communications. (See paragraph 6 of the Code.)

In 1963 the PRSA Board of Directors approved the interpretation of this Code as it applies to financial public relations practice which is defined as "that area of public relations which relates to the dissemination of information that affects the understanding of stockholders and investors generally concerning the financial position and prospects of a company, and includes among its objectives the improvement of relations between corporations and their stockholders." This interpretation which was prepared for the PRSA Board by the Society's Legal Counsel, an Advisory Committee working with the Securities and Exchange Commission and the PRSA Committee on Standards of Professional Practice is rooted directly in the Code and has the full force of the Code behind it. A violation of any one of the ten points should be subject to the same procedures and penalties as a violation of the Code.

CODE FOR PROFESSIONAL STANDARDS FOR THE PRACTICE OF PUBLIC RELATIONS

Declaration of Principles

Members of the Public Relations Society of America base their professional principles on the fundamental value and dignity of the individual, holding that the free exercise of human rights, especially freedom of speech, freedom of assembly and freedom of the press, is essential to the practice of public relations.

In serving the interests of clients and employers, we dedicate ourselves to the goals of better communication, understanding and cooperation among the diverse individuals, groups and institutions of society.

We pledge:

To conduct ourselves professionally, with truth, accuracy, fairness and responsibility to the public;

To improve our individual competence and advance the knowledge and proficiency of the profession through continuing research and education;

And to adhere to the articles of the Code of Professional Standards for the Practice of Public Relations as adopted by the governing Assembly of the Society.

Articles of the Code

These articles have been adopted by the Public Relations Society of America to promote and maintain high standards of public service and ethical conduct among its members.

1. A member shall deal fairly with clients or employers, past and present, with fellow practitioners and the general public.

2. A member shall conduct his or her professional life in accord with the public interest.

3. A member shall adhere to truth and accuracy and to generally accepted standards of good taste.

4.   A member shall not represent conflicting or competing interests without the express consent of those involved, given after a full disclosure of the facts; nor place himself or herself in a position where the member's interest is or may be in conflict with a duty to a client, or others, without a full disclosure of such interests to all involved.

5.   A member shall safeguard the confidences of both present and former clients or employers and shall not accept retainers or employment which may involve the disclosure or use of these confidences to the disadvantage or prejudice of such clients or employers.

6.   A member shall not engage in any practice which tends to corrupt the integrity of channels of communication or the processes of government.

7.   A member shall not intentionally communicate false or misleading information and is obligated to use care to avoid communication of false or misleading information.

8.   A member shall be prepared to identify publicly the name of the client or employer on whose behalf any public communication is made.

9.   A member shall not make use of any individual or organization purporting to serve or represent an announced cause, or purporting to be independent or unbiased, but actually serving an undisclosed special or private interest of a member, client or employer.

10.   A member shall not intentionally injure the professional reputation or practice of another practitioner. However, if a member has evidence that another member has been guilty of unethical, illegal or unfair practices, including those in violation of this Code, the member shall present the information promptly to the proper authorities of the Society for action in accordance with the procedure set forth in Article XIII of the Bylaws.

11.   A member called as a witness in a proceeding for the enforcement of this Code shall be bound to appear, unless excused for sufficient reason by the Judicial Panel.

12.   A member, in performing services for a client or employer, shall not accept fees, commissions or any other valuable consideration from anyone other than the client or employer in connection with those services without the express consent of the client or employer, given after a full disclosure of the facts.

13.   A member shall not guarantee the achievement of specified results beyond the member's direct control.

14.   A member shall, as soon as possible, sever relations with any organization or individual if such relationship requires conduct contrary to the articles of this Code.

Official Interpretations of the Code

Interpretation of Code Paragraph 2 which reads, "A member shall conduct his or her professional life in accord with the public interest."

The public interest is here defined primarily as comprising respect for and enforcement of the rights guaranteed by the Constitution of the United States of America.

Interpretation of Code Paragraph 5 which reads, "A member shall safeguard the confidences of both present and former clients or employers and shall not accept retainers or employment which may involve the disclosure or use of these confidences to the disadvantage or prejudice of such clients or employers."

This article does not prohibit a member who has knowledge of client or employer activities which are illegal from making such disclosures to the proper authorities as he or she believes are legally required.

Interpretation of Code Paragraph 6 which reads, "A member shall not engage in any practice which tends to corrupt the integrity of channels of communication or the processes of government."

1. Practices prohibited by this paragraph are those which tend to place representatives of media or government under an obligation to the member, or the member's employer or client, which is in conflict with their obligations to media or government, such as:

   a. the giving of gifts of more than nominal value;

   b. any form of payment or compensation to a member of the media in order to obtain preferential or guaranteed news or editorial coverage in the medium;

   c. any retainer or fee to a media employee or use of such employee if retained by a client or employer, where the circumstances are not fully disclosed to and accepted by the media employer;

   d. providing trips for media representatives which are unrelated to legitimate news interest;

   e. the use by a member of an investment or loan or advertising commitment made by the member, or the member's client or employer, to obtain preferential or guaranteed coverage in the medium.

2. This Code paragraph does not prohibit hosting media or government representatives at meals, cocktails, or news functions or special events which are occasions for the exchange of news information or views, or the

furtherance of understanding which is part of the public relations function. Nor does it prohibit the bona fide press event or tour when media or government representatives are given an opportunity for on-the-spot viewing of a newsworthy product, process or event in which the media or government representatives have a legitimate interest. What is customary or reasonable hospitality has to be a matter of particular judgment in specific situations. In all of these cases, however, it is or should be understood that no preferential treatment or guarantees are expected or implied and that complete independence always is left to the media or government representative.

3. This paragraph does not prohibit the reasonable giving or lending of sample products or services to media representatives who have a legitimate interest in the products or services.

Interpretation of Code Paragraph 13 which reads, "A member shall not guarantee the achievement of specified results beyond the member's direct control."

This Code paragraph, in effect, prohibits misleading a client or employer as to what professional public relations can accomplish. It does not prohibit guarantees of quality or service. But it does prohibit guaranteeing specific results which, by their very nature, cannot be guaranteed because they are not subject to the member's control. As an example, a guarantee that a news release will appear specifically in a particular publication would be prohibited. This paragraph should not be interpreted as prohibiting contingent fees.

An Official Interpretation of the Code as it Applies to
Political Public Relations

Preamble

In the practice of political public relations, a PRSA member must have professional capabilities to offer an employer or client quite apart from any political relationships of value, and members may serve their employer or client without necessarily having attributed to them the character, reputation or beliefs of those they serve. It is understood that members may choose to serve only those interests with whose political philosophy they are personally comfortable.

Definition

"Political Public Relations" is defined as those areas of public relations which relate to:

a. the counseling of political organizations, committees, candidates or potential candidates for public office; and groups constituted for the purpose of influencing the vote on any ballot issue;
b. the counseling of holders of public office;
c. the management, or direction, of a political campaign for or against a candidate for political office; or for or against a ballot issue to be determined by voter approval or rejection;
d. the practice of public relations on behalf of a client or an employer in connection with that client's or employer's relationships with any candidates or holders of public office with the purpose of influencing legislation or government regulation or treatment of a client or employer, regardless of whether the PRSA member is a recognized lobbyist;
e. the counseling of government bodies, or segments thereof, either domestic or foreign.

Precepts

1. It is the responsibility of PRSA members practicing political public relations, as defined above, to be conversant with the various statutes, local, state and federal, governing such activities and to adhere to them strictly. This includes, but is not limited to, the various local, state, and federal laws, court decisions and official interpretations governing lobbying, political contributions, disclosure, elections, libel, slander and the like. In carrying out this responsibility, members shall seek appropriate counseling whenever necessary.

2. It is also the responsibility of members to abide by PRSA's Code of Professional Standards.

3. Members shall represent clients or employers in good faith, and while partisan advocacy on behalf of a candidate or public issue may be expected, members shall act in accord with the public interest and adhere to truth and accuracy and to generally accepted standards of good taste.

4. Members shall not issue descriptive material or any advertising or publicity information or participate in the preparation or use thereof which is not signed by responsible persons or is false, misleading or unlabeled as to its source, and are obligated to use care to avoid dissemination of any such material.

5. Members have an obligation to clients to disclose what remuneration beyond their fees they expect to receive as a result of their relationship, such as commissions for media advertising, printing and the like, and should not accept such extra payment without their clients' consent.

6. Members shall not improperly use their positions to encourage additional future employment or compensation. It is understood that successful campaign directors or managers, because of the performance of their duties and the working relationship that develops, may well continue to assist and counsel, for pay, the successful candidate.

7. Members shall voluntarily disclose to employers or clients the identity of other employers or clients with whom they are currently associated and whose interests might be affected favorably or unfavorably by their political representation.

8. Members shall respect the confidentiality of information pertaining to employers or clients even after the relationships cease, avoiding future associations wherein insider information is sought that would give a desired advantage over a member's previous clients.

9. In avoiding practices which might tend to corrupt the processes of government, members shall not make undisclosed gifts of cash or other valuable considerations which are designed to influence specific decisions of voters, legislators or public officials on public matters. A business lunch or dinner, or other comparable expenditure made in the course of communicating a point of view or public position, would not constitute such a violation. Nor, for example, would a plant visit designed and financed to provide useful background information to an interested legislator or candidate.

10. Nothing herein should be construed as prohibiting members from making legal, properly disclosed contributions to the candidates, party or referenda issues of their choice.

11. Members shall not, through the use of information known to be false or misleading, conveyed directly or through a third party, intentionally injure the public reputation of an opposing interest.

An Official Interpretation of the Code as it Applies to Financial Public Relations

This interpretation of the Society Code as it applies to financial public relations was originally adopted in 1963 and amended in 1972 and 1977 by action of the PRSA Board of Directors. "Financial public relations" is defined as "that area of public relations which relates to the dissemination of information that affects the understanding of stockholders and investors generally concerning the financial position and prospects of a company, and includes among its objectives the improvement of relations between corporations and their stockholders." The interpretation was prepared in 1963 by the Society's Financial Relations Committee working with the Securities and Exchange Commission and with the advice of the Society's Legal Counsel. It is rooted directly in the Code with the full force of the Code behind it and a violation of any of the following paragraphs is subject to the same procedures and penalties as violation of the Code.

1. It is the responsibility of PRSA members who practice financial public relations to be thoroughly familiar with and understand the rules and regulations of the SEC and the laws which it administers, as well as other laws, rules and regulations affecting financial public relations, and to act in accordance with their letter and spirit. In carrying out this responsibility, members shall also seek legal counsel, when appropriate, on matters concerning financial public relations.

2. Members shall adhere to the general policy of making full and timely disclosure of corporate information on behalf of clients or employers. The information disclosed shall be accurate, clear and understandable. The purpose of such disclosure is to provide the investing public with all material information affecting security values or influencing investment decisions. In complying with the duty of full and timely disclosure, members shall present all material facts, including those adverse to the company. They shall exercise care to ascertain the facts and to disseminate only information which they believe to be accurate. They shall not knowingly omit information, the omission of which might make a release false or misleading. Under no circumstances shall members participate in any activity designed to mislead, or manipulate the price of a company's securities.

3. Members shall publicly disclose or release information promptly so as to avoid the possibility of any use of the information by any insider or third party. To that end, members shall make every effort to comply with the spirit and intent of the timely disclosure policies of the stock exchanges, NASD, and the Securities and Exchange Commission. Material information shall be made available to all on an equal basis.

4.   Members shall not disclose confidential information the disclosure of which might be adverse to a valid corporate purpose or interest and whose disclosure is not required by the timely disclosure provisions of the law. During any such period of non-disclosure members shall not directly or indirectly (a) communicate the confidential information to any other person or (b) buy or sell or in any other way deal in the company's securities where the confidential information may materially affect the market for the security when disclosed. Material information shall be disclosed publicly as soon as its confidential status has terminated or the requirement of timely disclosure takes effect.

5.   During the registration period, members shall not engage in practices designed to precondition the market for such securities. During registration the issuance of forecasts, projections, predictions about sales and earnings, or opinions concerning security values or other aspects of the future performance of the company, shall be in accordance with current SEC regulations and statements of policy. In the case of companies whose securities are publicly held, the normal flow of factual information to shareholders and the investing public shall continue during the registration period.

6.   Where members have any reason to doubt that projections have an adequate basis in fact, they shall satisfy themselves as to the adequacy of the projections prior to disseminating them.

7.   Acting in concert with clients or employers, members shall act promptly to correct false or misleading information or rumors concerning clients' or employers' securities or business whenever they have reason to believe such information or rumors are materially affecting investor attitudes.

8.   Members shall not issue descriptive materials designed or written in such a fashion as to appear to be, contrary to fact, an independent third party endorsement or recommendation of a company or a security. Whenever members issue material for clients or employers, either in their own names or in the name of someone other than clients or employers, they shall disclose in large type and in a prominent position on the face of the material the source of such material and the existence of the issuer's client or employer relationship.

9.   Members shall not use inside information for personal gain. However, this is not intended to prohibit members from making bona fide investments in their company's or client's securities insofar as they can make such investments without the benefit of material inside information.

10. Members shall not accept compensation which would place them in a position of conflict with their duty to a client, employer or the investing public. Members shall not accept stock options from clients or employers nor accept securities as compensation at a price below market price except as part of an overall plan for corporate employees.

11. Members shall act so as to maintain the integrity of channels of public communication. They shall not pay or permit to be paid to any publication

or other communications medium any consideration in exchange for publicizing a company, except through clearly recognizable paid advertising.

12. Members shall in general be guided by the PRSA Declaration of Principles and the PRSA Code of Professional Standards for the Practice of Public Relations of which this Code is an official interpretation.

This Code, adopted by the PRSA Assembly, replaces a similar Code of Professional Standards for the Practice of Public Relations previously in force since 1954 and strengthened by revisions in 1959, 1963 and 1977.

CODE OF PROFESSIONAL STANDARDS

FOR THE PRACTICE OF PUBLIC RELATIONS

Declaration of Principles

Members of the Public Relations Society of America base their professional principles on the fundamental value and dignity of the individual, holding that the free exercise of human rights, especially freedom of speech, freedom of assembly, and freedom of the press, is essential to the practice of public relations.

In serving the interests of clients and employers, we dedicate ourselves to the goals of better communication, understanding, and cooperation among the diverse individuals, groups, and institutions of society, and of equal opportunity of employment in the public relations profession.

We pledge:

To conduct ourselves professionally, with truth, accuracy, fairness, and responsibility to the public;

To improve our individual competence and advance the knowledge and proficiency of the profession through continuing research and education;

And to adhere to the articles of the Code of Professional Standards for the Practice of Public Relations as adopted by the governing Assembly of the Society.

Code of Professional Standards for the Practice of Public Relations

These articles have been adopted by the Public Relations Society of America to promote and maintain high standards of public service and ethical conduct among its members.

1. A member shall conduct his or her professional life in accord with the **public interest.**

2. A member shall exemplify high standards of **honesty and integrity** while carrying out dual obligations to a client or employer and to the democratic process.

112

3.   A member shall **deal fairly** with the public, with past or present clients or employers, and with fellow practitioners, giving due respect to the ideal of free inquiry and to the opinions of others.

4.   A member shall adhere to the highest standards of **accuracy and truth,** avoiding extravagant claims or unfair comparisons and giving credit for ideas and words borrowed from others.

5.   A member shall not knowingly disseminate **false or misleading information** and shall act promptly to correct erroneous communications for which he or she is responsible.

6.   A member shall not engage in any practice which has the purpose of **corrupting** the integrity of channels of communications or the processes of government.

7.   A member shall be prepared to **identify publicly** the name of the client or employer on whose behalf any public communication is made.

8.   A member shall not use any individual or organization professing to serve or represent an announced cause, or professing to be independent or unbiased, but actually serving another or **undisclosed interest.**

9.   A member shall not **guarantee the achievement** of specified results beyond the member's direct control.

10.   A member shall **not represent conflicting** or competing interests without the express consent of those concerned, given after a full disclosure of the facts.

11.   A member shall not place himself or herself in a position where the member's **personal interest is or may be in conflict** with an obligation to an employer or client, or others, without full disclosure of such interests to all involved.

12.   A member shall **not accept fees, commissions, gifts or any other consideration** from anyone except clients or employers for whom services are performed without their express consent, given after full disclosure of the facts.

13.   A member shall scrupulously safeguard the **confidences and privacy rights** of present, former, and prospective clients or employers.

14.   A member shall not intentionally **damage the professional reputation** or practice of another practitioner.

15.   If a member has evidence that another member has been guilty of unethical, illegal, or unfair practices, including those in violation of this Code, the member is obligated to present the information promptly to the proper authorities of the Society for action in accordance with the procedure set forth in Article XII of the Bylaws.

16. A member called as a witness in a proceeding for enforcement of this Code is obligated to appear, unless excused for sufficient reason by the judicial panel.

17. A member shall, as soon as possible, sever relations with any organization or individual if such relationship requires conduct contrary to the articles of this Code.

Official Interpretations of the Code

Interpretation of Code Paragraph 1, which reads, "A member shall conduct his or her professional life in accord with the public interest."

The public interest is here defined primarily as comprising respect for and enforcement of the rights guaranteed by the Constitution of the United States of America.

Interpretation of Code Paragraph 6, which reads, "A member shall not engage in any practice which has the purpose of corrupting the integrity of channels or communication or the processes of government."

1. Among the practices prohibited by this paragraph are those that tend to place representatives of media or government under any obligation to the member, or the member's employer or client, which is in conflict with their obligations to media or government, such as:

   a. the giving of gifts of more than nominal value;

   b. any form of payment or compensation to a member of the media in order to obtain preferential or guaranteed news or editorial coverage in the medium;

   c. any retainer or fee to a media employee or use of such employee if retained by a client or employer, where the circumstances are not fully disclosed to and accepted by the media employer;

   d. providing trips, for media representatives, that are unrelated to legitimate news interest;

   e. the use by a member of an investment or loan or advertising commitment made by the member, or the member's client or employer, to obtain preferential or guaranteed coverage in the medium.

2. This Code paragraph does not prohibit hosting media or government representatives at meals, cocktails, or news functions and special events that are occasions for the exchange of news information or views, or the furtherance of understanding, which is part of the public relations

function. Nor does it prohibit the bona fide press event or tour when media or government representatives are given the opportunity for an on-the-spot viewing of a newsworthy product, process, or event in which the media or government representatives have a legitimate interest. What is customary or reasonable hospitality has to be a matter of particular judgment in specific situations. In all of these cases, however, it is, or should be, understood that no preferential treatment or guarantees are expected or implied and that complete independence always is left to the media or government representative.

3.   This paragraph does not prohibit the reasonable giving or lending of sample products or services to media representatives who have a legitimate interest in the products or services.

4.   It is permissible, under Article 6 of the Code, to offer complimentary or discount rates to the media (travel writers, for example) if the rate is for business use and is made available to all writers. Considerable question exists as to the propriety of extending such rates for personal use.

Interpretation of Code Paragraph 9, which reads, "A member shall not guarantee the achievement of specified results beyond the member's direct control."

This Code paragraph, in effect, prohibits misleading a client or employer as to what professional public relations can accomplish. It does not prohibit guarantees of quality of service. But it does prohibit guaranteeing specific results which, by their very nature, cannot be guaranteed because they are not subject to the member's control. As an example, a guarantee that a news release will appear specifically in a particular publication would be prohibited. This paragraph should not be interpreted as prohibiting contingent fees.

Interpretation of Code Paragraph 13, which reads, "A member shall scrupulously safeguard the confidences and privacy rights of present, former, and prospective clients or employers."

1.   This article does not prohibit a member who has knowledge of client or employer activities that are illegal from making such disclosures to the proper authorities as he or she believes are legally required.

2.   Communications between a practitioner and client/employer are deemed to be confidential under Article 13 of the Code of Professional Standards. However, although practitioner/client/employer communications are considered confidential between the parties, such communications are not privileged against disclosure in a court of law.

3.   In the absence of any contractual arrangement, the client or employer legally owns the rights to papers or materials created for him.

115

Interpretation of Code Paragraph 14, which reads, "A member shall not intentionally damage the professional reputation or practice of another practitioner."

> Blind solicitation, on its face, is not prohibited by the Code. However, if the customer list were improperly obtained, or if the solicitation contained references reflecting adversely on the quality of current services, a complaint might be justified.

An Official Interpretation of the Code as It Applies to Political Public Relations

Preamble

In the practice of political public relations, a PRSA member must have professional capabilities to offer an employer or client quite apart from any political relationships of value, and members may serve their employer or client without necessarily having attributed to them the character, reputation, or beliefs of those they serve. It is understood that members may choose to serve only those interests with whose political philosophy they are personally comfortable.

Definition

"Political Public Relations" is defined as those areas of public relations that relate to:

a.   the counseling of political organizations, committees, candidates, or potential candidates for public office; and groups constituted for the purpose of influencing the vote on any ballot issue;

b.   the counseling of holders of public office;

c.   the management, or direction, of a political campaign for or against a candidate for political office; or for or against a ballot issue to be determined by voter approval or rejection;

d.   the practice of public relations on behalf of a client or an employer in connection with that client's or employer's relationships with any candidates or holders of public office, with the purpose of influencing legislation or government regulation or treatment of a client or employer, regardless of whether the PRSA member is a recognized lobbyist;

e.   the counseling of government bodies, or segments thereof, either domestic or foreign.

Precepts

1. It is the responsibility of PRSA members practicing political public relations, as defined above, to be conversant with the various statutes, local, state, and federal, governing such activities and to adhere to them strictly. This includes, but is not limited to, the various local, state, and federal laws, court decisions, and official interpretations governing lobbying, political contributions, disclosure, elections, libel, slander, and the like. In carrying out this responsibility, members shall seek appropriate counseling whenever necessary.

2. It is also the responsibility of members to abide by PRSA's Code for Professional Standards.

3. Members shall represent clients or employers in good faith, and while partisan advocacy on behalf of a candidate or public issue may be expected, members shall act in accord with the public interest and adhere to truth and accuracy and to generally accepted standards of good taste.

4. Members shall not issue descriptive material or any advertising or publicity information or participate in the preparation or use thereof that is not signed by responsible persons or is false, misleading, or unlabeled as to its source, and are obligated to use care to avoid dissemination of any such material.

5. Members have an obligation to clients to disclose what remuneration beyond their fees they expect to receive as a result of their relationship, such as commissions for media advertising, printing, and the like, and should not accept such extra payment without their client's consent.

6. Members shall not improperly use their positions to encourage additional future employment or compensation. It is understood that successful campaign directors or managers, because of the performance of their duties and the working relationship that develops, may well continue to assist and counsel, for pay, the successful candidate.

7. Members shall voluntarily disclose to employers or clients the identity of other employers or clients with whom they are currently associated, and whose interests might be affected favorably or unfavorably by their political representation.

8. Members shall respect the confidentiality of information pertaining to employers or clients past, present, potential, even after the relationships cease, avoiding future associations wherein insider information is sought that would give a desired advantage over a member's previous clients.

9. In avoiding practices that might tend to corrupt the processes of government, members shall not make undisclosed gifts of cash or other valuable considerations that are designed to influence specific decisions of voters, legislators, or public officials on public matters. A business lunch or dinner, or other comparable expenditure made in the course of communicating a point of view or public position, would not constitute

such a violation. Nor, for example, would a plant visit designed and financed to provide useful background information to an interested legislator or candidate.

10. Nothing herein should be construed as prohibiting members from making legal, properly disclosed contributions to the candidates, party, or referenda issues of their choice.

11. Members shall not, through use of information known to be false or misleading, conveyed directly or through a third party, intentionally injure the public reputation of an opposing interest.

Adopted by the PRSA Assembly in 1988

An Official Interpretation of the Code
As It Applies to Financial Public Relations

The interpretation of the Society Code as it applies to financial public relations was originally adopted in 1963 and amended in 1972, 1977, 1983, and 1988 by action of the PRSA Board of Directors. "Financial public relations" is defined as "that area of public relations which relates to the dissemination of information that affects the understanding of stockholders and investors generally concerning the financial position and prospects of a company, and includes among its objectives the improvement of relations between corporations and their stockholders." The interpretation was prepared in 1963 by the Society's Financial Relations Committee, working with the Securities and Exchange Commission and with the advice of the Society's legal counsel. It is rooted directly in the Code with the full force of the Code behind it, and a violation of any of the following paragraphs is subject to the same procedures and penalties as violation of the Code.

1. It is the responsibility of PRSA members who practice financial public relations to be thoroughly familiar with and understand the rules and regulations of the SEC and the laws it administers, as well as other laws, rules, and regulations affecting financial public relations, and to act in accordance with their letter and spirit. In carrying out this responsibility, members shall also seek legal counsel, when appropriate, on matters concerning financial public relations.

2. Members shall adhere to the general policy of making full and timely disclosure of corporate information on behalf of clients or employers. The information disclosed shall be accurate, clear, and understandable. The purpose of such disclosure is to provide the investing public with all material information affecting security values or influencing investment

118

decisions. In complying with the duty of full and timely disclosure, members shall present all material facts, including those adverse to the company. They shall exercise care to ascertain the facts and to disseminate only information they believe to be accurate. They shall not knowingly omit information, the omission of which might make a release false or misleading. Under no circumstances shall members participate in any activity designed to mislead or manipulate the price of a company's securities.

3. Members shall publicly disclose or release information promptly so as to avoid the possibility of any use of the information by any insider or third party. To that end, members shall make every effort to comply with the spirit and intent of the timely-disclosure policies of the stock exchanges, NASD, and the SEC. Material information shall be made available on an equal basis.

4. Members shall not disclose confidential information the disclosure of which might be adverse to a valid corporate purpose or interest and whose disclosure is not required by the timely-disclosure provisions of the law. During any such period of non-disclosure members shall not directly or indirectly (as) communicate the confidential information to any other person or (b) buy or sell or in any other way deal in the company's securities where the confidential information may materially affect the market for the security when disclosed. Material information shall be disclosed publicly as soon as its confidential status has terminated or the requirement of timely disclosure takes effect.

5. During the registration period, members shall not engage in practices designed to precondition the market for such securities. During registration, the issuance of forecasts, projections, predictions about sales and earnings, or opinions concerning security values or other aspects of the future performance of the company, shall be in accordance with current SEC regulations and statements of policy. In the case of companies whose securities are publicly held, the normal flow of factual information to shareholders and the investing public shall continue during the registration period.

6. Where members have any reason to doubt that projections have an adequate basis in fact, they shall satisfy themselves as to the adequacy of the projections prior to disseminating them.

7. Acting in concert with clients or employers, members shall act promptly to correct false or misleading information or rumors concerning clients' or employers' securities or business whenever they have reason to believe such information or rumors are materially affecting investor attitudes.

8. Members shall not issue descriptive materials designed or written in such a fashion as to appear to be, contrary to fact, an independent third-party endorsement or recommendation of a company or a security. Whenever members issue material for clients or employers, either in their own names or in the name of someone other than clients or employers, they shall

119

disclose in large type and in a prominent position on the face of the material the source of such material and the existence of the issuer's client or employer relationship.

9. Members shall not use inside information for personal gain. However, this is not intended to prohibit members from making bona fide investments in their company's or client's securities insofar as they can make such investments without the benefit of material inside information.

10. Members shall not accept compensation that would place them in a position of conflict with their duty to a client, employer, or the investing public. Members shall not accept stock options from clients or employers nor accept securities as compensation at a price below market price except as part of an overall plan for corporate employees.

11. Members shall act so as to maintain the integrity of channels of public communication. They shall not pay or permit to be paid to any publication or other communications medium any consideration in exchange for publicizing a company, except through clearly recognizable paid advertising.

12. Members shall in general be guided by the PRSA Declaration of Principles and the Code of Professional Standards for the Practice of Public Relations of which this is an official interpretation.

Index

Note: References are to entry numbers, not pages. Names are indexed only if they serve as subjects in entries; for authors, check alphabetical bibliography.

The Editors

John P. Ferré is an associate professor of communication at the University of Louisville. He earned a B.A. in religion at Mars Hill College, an M.A. in communication at Purdue University, an M.A. in divinity at the University of Chicago, and a Ph.D. in communications at the University of Illinois at Urbana-Champaign. His books include *Rhetorical Patterns: An Anthology of Contemporary Essays*, *Merrill Guide to the Research Paper*, *A Social Gospel for Millions: The Religious Bestsellers of Charles Sheldon, Charles Gordon, and Harold Bell Wright*, and *Channels of Belief: Religion and American Commercial Television*.

Shirley C. Willihnganz is an associate professor of communication at the University of Louisville. She earned a B.A. in psychology and journalism and an M.A. in speech communication at Wayne State University, and a Ph.D. in speech communication at the University of Illinois at Urbana-Champaign. Before pursuing an academic career, she worked as an alcoholism counselor, reporter, photographer, and manager of public relations. She has published articles in *Central States Speech Journal*, *Communication Education*, *Health Education Quarterly*, *Journal of Applied Communication Research*, and *Management Communication Quarterly*.